TRANSITIONING MILITARY

CYBERSECURITY PROFESSIONAL

To Steve -
Thanks for
all your support -
enjoy the journey!

Sandy
Lawrence

THE TRANSITIONING MILITARY SERIES

THE TRANSITIONING MILITARY CYBERSECURITY PROFESSIONAL

Dr. Ray A. Letteer, CISSP, C|CISO
LTC Jay Hicks, Ret, PMP
Sandy Cobb, PfMP, PgMP, PMP

GR8TRANSITIONS4U, INC.

Published by GR8TRANSITIONS4U
GR8TRANSITIONS4U (USA) Inc.
PO Box 495
Valrico, FL 33595

Letteer, Ray
Hicks, Jay
Cobb, Sandy
THE TRANSITIONING CYBERSECURITY PROFESSIONAL
Includes End Notes
ISBN 978-0-9864376-5-6

Printed in the United States of America
Book design by Tamara Parsons
Kensington Type & Graphics

Dedicated to the Soldiers,
Sailors, Airmen, and Marines
of the United States Military.

In honor of the memory of my mother,
Jean Rose Letteer, whose love for books and learning
lit the fire in my heart so many years ago.

Table of Contents

Foreword

In an era where information is the "new gold," the cyber security profession is a discipline that requires the best and brightest minds we can attract across a broad range of technical and social science disciplines. The demand for highly qualified cyber security professionals in government, industry, and academia is growing at a rapid rate. Unfortunately, supply doesn't begin to meet the demand.

In The Transitioning Military Cyber Security Professional, Dr. Letteer and his team have performed a valuable service for transitioning military service members. In an era of constant change, confusion, complexity, and misinformation, they have clearly and succinctly laid out a well written and easy to follow career guide with tools that provide keen insights into the cyber security profession and its expanding role.

The book is an important guide not only for those currently in the cyber security profession, but those who are considering entering the field. It highlights the often understated qualities and traits that our men and women in uniform bring to the job market. Further, it provides helpful suggestions in leveraging those skills and qualities in their job search and beyond. There is a highly useful description and career path for the various different opportunities in the cyber security field. The book is replete with examples, useful tips, and suggestions. It also shows, in a thoughtful manner, the steps and qualifications leading to career advancement. Included is a flexible roadmap in career progression. Helpful questions, figures, and tables, ensure that one fully considers the key aspects along the career path of the cyber security professional.

By focusing on transitioning military members and the strong leadership skills they have honed, this book transcends other career guides. It will ease the transition and relieve much of the angst as one prepares for their next career in cybersecurity. It is a must read for anyone departing military service and considering a cybersecurity career.

Lt. Gen. Robert M. Shea, USMC (Ret.)
Chief Executive Officer
Armed Forces Communications and
Electronics Association (AFCEA) International

CONGRATULATIONS! If you have picked up this book, you are probably ready to embark on your military transition. You may be unaware of the amount of exposure to the cybersecurity career field you have gained from the military. This book will assist with military transitional challenges and provide some good common sense guidance as you deal with the uncertainties and the associated ambiguities along your journey. By reading and using the tactics in this book, you gain a professional advantage, setting into motion a course of action that will reduce transitional stress and create a satisfying and financially lucrative outcome.

Millions of service members have transitioned – now it is your turn. This book, along with its companion guide, will organize the chaos associated with transition, ease your concerns and increase your confidence. Go now and down load your free companion guide from Gr8MilitaryCyber.com. This guide contains copies of reusable assessments, charting forms and a personal strategic roadmap, in addition to process details and examples for using the forms. Keep the companion guide nearby and use it when performing the personal assessments and charting your strategic roadmap. Leverage your military experience.

Good luck in your transition!

THE TRANSITIONING MILITARY CYBERSECURITY PROFESSIONAL

1

Introduction

IT ALL STARTED WITH A 75 CENT ACCOUNTING ERROR. While the first generation of computers was developed in the 1940s, the development of transistors, integrated circuits, and eventually microprocessors helped transform business and science. In the case of the accounting error in 1986 at Lawrence Berkley National Laboratory, cybersecurity and the related tactics, techniques, and procedures arguably had its birth. Clifford Stoll, an astrophysicist whose grant had ended, took over managing the computer systems for the lab and was tracking the usage accounts when he discovered a 75 cent error in a $2,387 monthly bill. Ever the curious mind, Dr. Stoll began researching the problem to determine what would have caused the shortfall. After determining it wasn't a programming error, he began digging deeper into the audit processes and usage logs to discover that someone had "hacked" into the lab's systems. Two years later, he traced the "hacker" to a German citizen named Marcus Hess, who had been hired by Hungarian intelligence to

> "*The quality of decision is like the well-timed swoop of a falcon which enables it to strike...*"
>
> **Sun Tzu 孫子**
> *The Art of War*

break into US and NATO computer systems. Dr. Stoll's approach to solve the problem was based upon scientific processes, attention to detail, an inquisitive nature, and developing relationships with other organizations. He developed what could arguably be the first "honey pot" or special network that appears to be a legitimate site or network, but is really an isolated and controlled monitoring capability, establishing the first organized security audit trail review for systems administrators. Cliff discovered that the version of the Unix operating system used by the lab – and most of the scientific, academic, and government, – had a series of flaws that could be easily compromised. This entire episode was described in Clifford Stoll's book, *The Cuckcoo's Egg,* published in 1989.

It didn't take long for another major cybersecurity incident to occur. On November 2, 1988, the first computer worm was unleashed on the Internet. Robert Morris, Jr. had discovered the same set of Unix flaws that Dr. Stoll had found, and created a worm to attempt to measure the Internet. An unintended consequence was that the worm would keep re-infecting the systems, causing a significant denial of service effect. What this revealed – besides the Unix vulnerabilities – was that the many systems administrators around the world had no common response processes, no common communication medium (they used email, and that was shut down when the worm shut down the system), and no centralized ability to report and share experiences. Robert Morris, Jr. was convicted under the relatively new law, the Computer Fraud and Abuse Act (1986). This incident solidified the need for a national Computer Emergency Response Team or CERT, and started us down the path that perhaps our computer systems are more vulnerable than we thought. These two examples really didn't impact the average person in the 1980s. It was interesting news, but in reality no one had a computer at home at that time. For most, this seemed like a curiosity, at best.

Now we flash forward to today. Many of us can't remember a time when we didn't have a computer, whether it was a work computer, a personal computer, or both. For others, we are still in the mind-set of the 1980s, when computers really weren't part of our lives and information technology (IT) was just a science fiction career. We might still have issues working with computers, not really understanding what happens inside them and are sometimes reminded how "to err is human; but to really foul things up, it takes a computer." Marc Prensky categorized us as either "digital natives" – those born after 1980 and who grew up with IT and on-line experience; and "digital immigrants" – those born before 1980 and had to learn to use IT as a new aspect of life.[1]

There are many who are reading this book that might actually remember the IBM® Selectric Typewriter as the communication technology of choice in the office. Others may have experience with computers limited to only social media interaction, the occasional on-line gaming experience of choice, or to do research on-line and type up home-work assignments. To put it frankly, our experience with IT and computers has had a rapid rise over the past 30 years.

In 2007, the Department of Defense (DoD) formally declared cyberspace to be a new war-fighting domain, changing that description finally in 2011, calling cyberspace "...an *operational domain* to organize, train, and equip so that DoD can take full advantage of cyberspace's potential"[2] because, quite honestly, it looked like we were trying to militarize the Internet. In whatever manner it is defined, many of you have had experience with and depended upon IT systems that provided supply information that assured the right fuel or other commodities were provided, managed and reported command and control data, and ensured pay and medical services were delivered – in short, you made sure the mission was accomplished using information systems and following cybersecurity principles.

Change

Nothing is constant, except change. The Lawrence Berkley National Lab hacking and the Morris worm show how fast change can occur. It only takes a minute to see how our tools and systems change "at the speed of the Internet" to deeply appreciated the situation. Many of you had your careers change, probably due to the new tools you could use on information systems. Now you are going to change occupations and potential career fields. In today's tumultuous work environment, modern workers must be flexible, be able to adapt to change, and reinvent themselves every few years to remain viable. The good news is that you have spent years learning to adapt to ever changing environments while in the military. You know that your military experience has instilled the ability to be flexible and given you the ability to respond to change.

Why Cybersecurity?

To start, cybersecurity has become a critical, national goal over the past few years. Cybersecurity has become so important in the Federal government that a cross-agency priority goal was established. The cybersecurity goal statement is "Improve cybersecurity performance through ongoing awareness of information security, vulnerabilities, and threats impacting the operating information environment, ensuring that only authorized users have access to resources and information; and the implementation of technologies and processes that reduce the risk of malware."[3]

Your future career path could very well be cybersecurity. PYMNTS.com, one of the largest business-to-business (B2B) commercial transactions platforms for the payments industry, noted that the cybersecurity market could grow from $105 billion in 2015 to as much as $170 billion by 2020. They note that this growth trend of a high demand for cybersecurity professionals is driven by the ever-growing threat of cybercriminals and other sources of cyber-attack. They quote MarketResearch.com predicting the cybersecurity market in North America alone will increase at a compound annual growth rate (CAGR) of 7.32 percent over the period of 2014–2019.[4]

Michael Brown, CEO at Symantec, told Forbes that the demand for cybersecurity professionals is expected to rise globally to 6 million by 2019, with a projected shortage of 1.5 million.[5] The National Institute of Standards and Technology (NIST) posted a graphic, depicting the demand for the Cybersecurity Workforce.[6] As you can see in Figure 1.1, there is an estimated need of 1.5 million cybersecurity professionals needed by 2020. It takes longer to fill cybersecurity positions, because there are so few qualified candidates. Skill sets in programming languages and processes, such as auditing and testing, are in demand. Some of the skills hardest to fill are in system administration, compliance, forensics, and cloud capabilities, such as Platform-as-a-Service (PaaS). The Federal Government hired 3,000 new cybersecurity and IT professionals in the first 6 months of fiscal year 2016. However, federal agencies say there is clearly more work to do, and are committed to a plan by which Federal agencies will hire thousands of individuals to fill critical cybersecurity and IT positions each year for the foreseeable future.

Cybersecurity Work Force Demand

1.5 Million
Cybersecurity Professionals Needed To accommodate Shortfall by 2020

Approximately 10%
of current cybersecurity workforce are comprised of women

Biggest Skills Gap
72% - Ability to Understand Business
46% - Technical Skills
42% - Communication Skills

Roles In Demand
- Information Security
- Network Setup
- Auditing
- Network Protocols
- Core Database, Coding and Scripting
- Systems Administration

1.5 Million
Cybersecurity Professionals Needed To accommodate Shortfall by 2020

On Average, 52%
of IT professionals surveyed stated fewer than 25% of all applicants were qualified

Fastest Growing Job Skills
- Python
- HIPPA
- Risk Management
- Internal Auditing
- Audit Planning

18% Growth
Computer and mathematical will grow much faster than the average job during 2012-2024

nist.gov/nice

Figure 1.1 | Cybersecurity Workforce Demand

Experts in the field believe that military are well suited for the career field of cybersecurity. Your leadership and planning skills ingrained during military service, and your adaptability to change, will enable you to successfully transition into a great career field like cybersecurity. Communications officer, cybersecurity technician, network planning officer, air command & control systems officer, cyberspace operations officer, and cyber systems operations specialists are all examples of military terms that equate to cybersecurity in the commercial world. Combined with the specialized training one can receive in the military, and the high demand for personnel working in the field, all make cybersecurity a high-value, target rich environment for you to consider.

You may not fully understand the commercial terminology and methodologies, but you will be highly successful once you grasp these concepts and see how your military experience has prepared you for them. Your skill sets need to be translated and repackaged so that hiring managers spot your capabilities. Fortunately, you already know and understand the basics of cybersecurity. The military has exposed you to annual cybersecurity training. You had to learn about access control through the use of the Common Access Card and other alternate tokens. If you've ever lost data on a system, you probably also learned the principle of backing up data and have a contingency or disaster recovery plan for your systems.

You have also learned the discipline of time management, how to work a multitude of simultaneous requirements, and how to get the job accomplished. Further, you know how to take charge when required, are not afraid to lead, and know how to talk to senior leadership. All of these essential skills that you have already acquired are discussed later as critical attributes and increasing your understanding of cybersecurity implementation and support.

Transition Strategy

As a military service member, you inherently understand planning and strategy. Using this skill to plan and execute a personal strategy during your transition is potentially your greatest attribute. Knowing the tactics needed to get you to your goals and objectives is key. As you transition from the military, you should start asking questions like:

1. How do I chart a course of action that will allow me to unleash my superb capabilities as quickly as possible after transitioning from the military?
2. Do I know my best qualities to exploit for my next career?
3. Do I know what career is best suited for me?
4. How do I get from where I am to where I want to be?

Throughout this book, you will build your own 'personal strategic roadmap' (PSR) to organize your thoughts and establish your way ahead for a successful transition. Your 'PSR' will assist in answering these types of questions, providing success in your career change by establishing obtainable goals and objectives. Interestingly, this process is quite natural for both the military mind and that of the cybersecurity professional.

The Value of This Book

Most transition programs offer general guidance by means of generically creating a resume, interview tips, and similar features. You become acutely aware of the transition challenge when you discover the uncertainties associated with career path decisions. It can take years to decide on a path if you do not have an understanding of who you are, what qualities and capabilities you offer, what you desire from life and where you yearn to live.

Key to this books value is that it helps drive a career path choice based upon your capabilities, experience, family needs and desires. This book is uniquely suited to help you answer those questions and guide you to the best-suited career path for you and your family. Quality information and assessment tools in this book will help you evaluate your current situation and enable the development of a personal strategic roadmap for your successful transition. A series of personal inventory questions are provided in the areas of environment, characteristics, timing, career field, and desired market place. Personal factors in these assessments focus upon your internal makeup, while others help organize your desires with regard to external factors, as depicted in Figure 1.2.

> ***"Strategy without tactics is the slowest route to victory. Tactics without strategy is the noise before defeat."***
>
> **Sun Tzu 孫子**
> ***The Art of War***

Personal Assessments

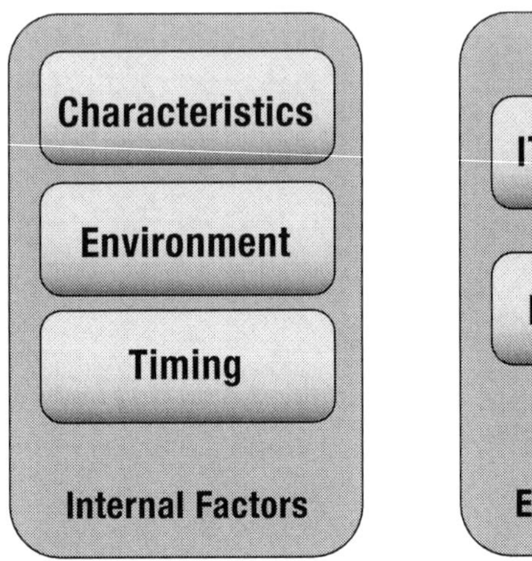

Figure 1.2 | Personal Assessments

Through this series of questions and the use of their results, a personal score for each assessment is derived. All scores align to build your strategic roadmap and guide you toward a potential career path in a marketable area that you and your family will find satisfying and rewarding. Further, this roadmap will prove invaluable, as it has incorporated your motivations, skillsets and willingness to seek out the wide variety of opportunities in your next career as a cybersecurity professional. Regardless of your path, this book will help you understand your strengths and weaknesses while increasing your professional skills and making yourself more marketable.

The next section provides a detailed look at each chapter and the assistance needed to develop your personal strategic roadmap.

Know Yourself *(Chapter 2)*

Chapter 2 begins with where you are now in the military, and discusses common challenges you may face during your transition. After thought provoking reviews of attributes and skills common to many in the military, you will gain an understanding of the importance of your existing cyber and IT skills and how they map to the military cybersecurity and IT career fields (Figure 1.3). This mapping will play in an important role in Chapter 3, as we continue to map your skills to commercial cybersecurity occupations.

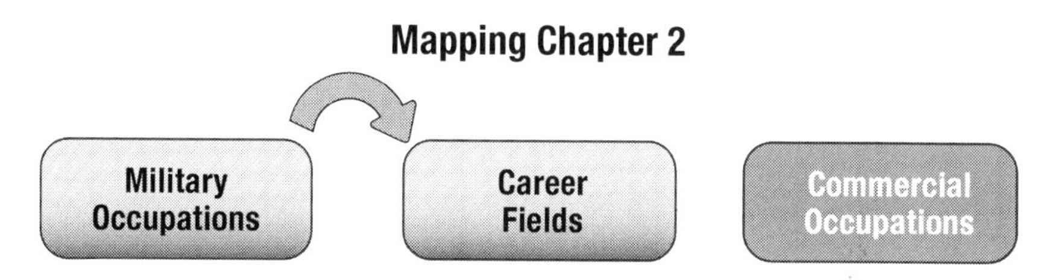

Figure 1.3 | Mapping Military Occupations to Career Fields

Multiple assessments covering personal and environmental desires are given in this chapter. Through these self-assessments you will gain a documented understanding of your desires as they relate to your transition. Partner or spouse participation in this chapter is recommended, as any transition should be a team decision.

Cybersecurity Profession Basics *(Chapter 3)*

You have already performed many cyber roles, just not commercially. In this chapter, you will gain an understanding of the commercial vernacular needed to assist your transition and better position yourself for a career in cybersecurity. From the mapping of your military skills to cybersecurity core functions addressed in Chapter 2, you will be introduced to the cybersecurity career field aligned within various categories. These categories are further elaborated into roles with specific examples of job titles, creating the final step to connect-the-dots between military experience and commercial jobs (Figure 1.4). This innovative and unique approach offered in *The Transitioning Military Series* provides a standardized and no-nonsense approach to translate your military skills into viable, realistic and sensible career opportunities.

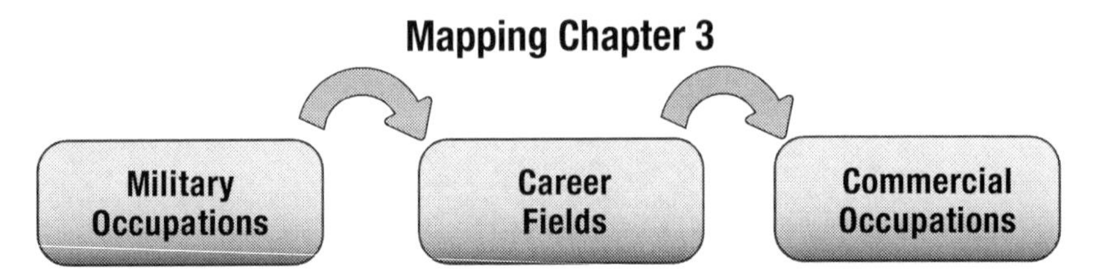

Figure 1.4 | Mapping military to commercial career fields and occupations

Through this chapter you will gain an insider's perspective on career paths, sample job descriptions and corresponding roles/duties. For those wanting to gain that extra edge, we explore educational opportunities as well as listing different types of certifications that you can pursue to include cost, and expected return on investment. A crosswalk of terminology, resources and the basics of commercial cybersecurity will help frame careers that you may be interested in pursuing.

The Market Place *(Chapter 4)*

This chapter looks at three markets for the cybersecurity professional after the service: Department of Defense (DoD) contracting, civil service and commercial (or corporate). Obviously, there are significant differences between military and commerical markets. Many of the different characteristics are presented, outlining pros and cons of each market. Entrepreneurship and Federally Funded Research and Development Centers (FFRDC) and University Affiliated Research Centers (UARC) are briefly discussed. A marketplace assessment will help guide you through a process to assist you in determining your risk tolerance, job creativity, income needs, and stress levels.

The Right Fit *(Chapter 5)*

Assessment results will be organized and analyzed resulting in a personal index, unfolding your personal roadmap, plotting your best-suited career transition. Key indicators from your environmental, characteristics, skills, timing, and marketplace assessments will become clearly stated tactics supporting your roadmap. With this information and tactics in hand, you will develop options to pursue given your strategic goals and objectives. Executing your personal strategic roadmap will be key to finding and pursuing the best transition path and job based on your assessment results.

Conventions used in this Book

Each chapter highlights common challenges and provides additional resources for your personal growth. Throughout the book, the star box shown here is used to call your attention to important facts to further investigate and use for transition. Sources vary from websites, book references, credentialing materials, or other programs and resources in the area of military or commerical cybersecurity.

Success Stories

Each chapter has an associated Success story from veterans that have come before you; providing encouragement during your transition to commercial cybersecurity.

Appendices and Website

Our goal with this book is to help you assess and organize key facets of your life and experiences that will point you towards the best, most lucrative and rewarding career in cybersecurity. This book and website provide a repository of easily accessible resources and experiences to assist you in your transition. Tools, assessments and templates are available in the appendices. Having purchased this book, you are also eligible for the Companion Guide, where reusable tools and templates are provided in electronic format online through the Gr8MilitaryCyber.com website.

Regardless of the path you choose, use this book and the associated assessment tools from each chapter, as a system to assist you in compiling your personal strategic roadmap as a guide to finding the most effective course of action for your transition.

The only question remaining is: Have you thought of everything you need to make the right decision? Let's find out!

Jimmy Clevenger
Accident drives cyber skills

JIMMY JOINED THE MARINE CORPS IN 1998 AND WAS TRAINED IN AIR DEFENSE COMMAND AND CONTROL SYSTEMS, INITIALLY AS AN AIR CONTROL ELECTRONICS OPERATOR (MOS 7234) AND LATER AS A TACTICAL AIR DEFENSE CONTROLLER (MOS 7236). During his time in the Marine Corps, Jimmy deployed all over the world as an aviation command and control Marine and became a fully combat qualified senior air director. As an enlisted Marine Sergeant, he was sent to aid in generating the air defense planning for the invasion of Iraq and was the only enlisted individual involved in that effort. While operating air defense command and control systems, Jimmy became an expert on how the system worked across the Open System Interconnection (OSI) stack and began his journey into integrating new technologies and exploiting systems as he worked on various deployments. In 2003 after returning home from the invasion of Iraq, Jimmy was involved in a vehicle accident that resulted in two broken vertebrae in his lower back. Knowing his military career was soon to be over, Jimmy began researching career forecasts published by the Bureau of Labor and Statics, and noticed information security was predicted to be the fastest growing career field over the next 20 years. He decided to go back to school and obtain a degree in the field, getting and Associate of Applied Science in Computer Information Systems (IT/Network Security Management), followed later with a Bachelor of Science and a Master of Science degrees in management information systems, both with a concentration in security management. Before his medical discharge in 2007, Jimmy was selected to join a staff established by the deputy commandant for aviation to evaluate new doctrine opportunities based on technology advances in the air command and control community. He spent his time honing his system exploitation skills from 2003 to 2007, which gained him a foot hold in the cybersecurity workforce when he transitioned out of the USMC. Jimmy worked for two years as a government contractor, which included positions as a principal analyst, project officer, to program manager. He also worked as a system security officer for a major system as an additional duty. Jimmy came into the government in 2009 to specifically lead an aggressive effort to change Marine Corps engineer culture to embrace cybersecurity engineering holistically, resulting in obtaining an approval to operate for his program 18 months ahead of schedule and 35% under the planned cybersecurity engineering budget. In 2012, Jimmy was promoted to take over the certification and accreditation (C&A) branch within Marine Corps Systems Command (MCSC), and two years later was promoted again where he serves today as the system security engineering division director and as the senior certification authority for MCSC.

2

Know Yourself

SUCCESSFUL TRANSITION STARTS WITH KNOWING YOURSELF. Part of this understanding is an awareness of your personal environmental factors and a keen sense of timing in order to make your next move. Knowing yourself and exploiting your strengths are the best ways to acknowledge your level of readiness for transition.

This chapter is an exploration of you and why you are desirable in the commercial world as a cybersecurity professional. Most successful transitions occur when you align your desires with your traits, attributes and characteristics to the job market. Identifying your undiscovered corporate abilities and applying them to your resume and interview performance will increase your probability of a successful transition.

> *"The most difficult thing in life is to know yourself"*
> ~ Greek Philosopher Thales

To get started, here are a few initial thoughts to get you thinking about how your desires relate to the cybersecurity career field. Do you like to develop, create, maintain, and write or code new (or modify existing) computer applications, software, or specialized utility programs? Do you like the idea of conducting independent comprehensive assessments of the management, operational, and technical security controls of IT to determine the overall effectiveness of those controls? If you can say "yes" to either of these, then the **Securely Provision** roles may be of interest to you.

Does the idea of developing cyberspace workforce plans, strategies and guidance to support cyberspace workforce manpower, personnel, training and education requirements appeal to you? Does developing cyberspace plans, strategy and policy to support and align with organizational cyberspace missions and initiatives seem interesting? If so, then the **Oversee & Govern** roles might be an option.

Does the work of using data collected from a variety of cyber defense tools (e.g., intrusion detection system alerts, firewalls, network traffic logs) to analyze events that occur within their environments for the purposes of mitigating threats; or testing, implementing, deploying, maintaining, and administering the infrastructure hardware and software appeal to you as a career? If any of these seem genuinely appealing, then the **Protect & Defend** roles may be a career choice.

These are just a few of the specific work responsibilities in cybersecurity. If you want to jump to Chapter 3, you can read more about them in detail. The important point to remember is that before you start the broader steps described here in Chapter 2 to transition from the military, be very sure this is the career you want to have in the future. There are many who have fallen for the image of the cybersecurity professional (and there are many in movies and books from which to draw), only to discover it is not easy nor was it what was initially envisioned.

Honest introspection is not an easy task, but will prove valuable through this exercise. Three personal assessments are given in this very important chapter to help gain insight to your level of readiness (Figure 2.1). They include:

A **Characteristics Assessment** to gain an understanding of your military and undiscovered skills that will translate well to the cybersecurity career field.

An **Environmental Assessment** that will challenge your understanding on outside factors such as location, retirement, family, schools and faith. If you are married or have a significant other, it is highly recommended you both take the assessment. Afterwards, discuss any results that might warrant more detailed analysis to offer better alignment.

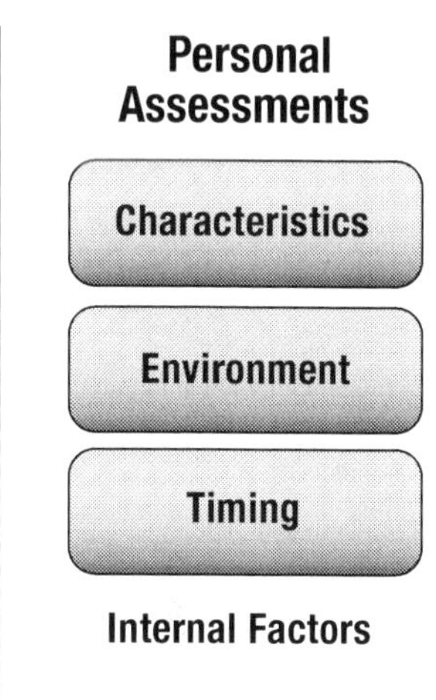

Figure 2.1 | Assessments

A **Timing Assessment** to determine how ready you are for transition, based upon the availability of time for planning or need for immediate action. As in any transition, analyzing the timing of your departure is a key factor. With regard to your timing, this chapter includes an analysis of many elements, such as studying the educational benefits, developing and refining your resume, making interview preparations and approaching certification in the cybersecurity field.

Desirability of Military Personnel in the Commercial Market

Employers find the characteristics and attributes obtained from your military experience invaluable. Transitioning military of all ranks have marketable technical and leadership skills. Your military experience has enhanced numerous attributes or core competencies including loyalty, respect, integrity, reliability, and team building. From a military perspective, you have led teams and have learned how to adapt rapidly to many different situations. As a team player, you know the weakest link is someone who needs help keeping the team moving forward. Additionally, as part of a military group, you are educated and technically savvy, a quick learner, drug free, possess a security clearance, perform well under pressure, and are familiar with relocation for advancement.

These attributes make you very marketable to an employer in the commercial market.[1]

Department of Defense (DoD) contract and civil service environments desire your military characteristics as well. Your understanding of military policy and procedure are vital to the defense contract organization. The bottom line is that you have many career options after the military, which are further discussed in Chapter Four. Your challenge is to consider job market opportunities and decide what you would like to do for your next career based on the proper alignment of your skills.

You need to remember, while your service time will help get your foot in the door for an interview, it will not get you the job. Going to interviews unprepared or being unqualified – regardless of your service time – will not get a return call, a second interview with management, or the job! Many potential employers today really have no idea what a Major, Chief Warrant Officer, Sergeant, or Private First Class really is. What employers want to see and understand is what you can do for them, how you will help their business or mission, or what you can tangibly produce to help their bottom-line. You need to be able to clearly and confidently convey your experience and knowledge, showing how your value will benefit them. Have the confidence to know that your skills and abilities from the service are directly applicable to the cybersecurity career field and job market. Translating these capabilities to the commercial employer is critical for your successful transition and the remainder of this chapter will provide assistance in this vital process.

Empirical Studies

Literally hundreds of companies are military friendly. The United States Automobile Association (USAA) hires veterans of all ranks and is perhaps one of the most veteran friendly companies in America today. Railroads such as Union Pacific and CSX have a tradition of being military friendly. Of course there are numerous defense contracting companies (L-3, General Dynamics,

Booze | Allen | Hamilton, Lockheed Martin, CACI, etc.) that frequently hire former military personnel as well.[2]

A survey was recently published by the Society for Human Resource Managers on the subject of employers and their thoughts on hiring former military personnel. The survey was given to Human Resource professionals from across many different U.S. based companies. The findings were startling. Many companies felt that there are many benefits to recruiting and hiring veterans. The most commonly cited quality is a sense of responsibility and ability to see efforts through to completion. In fact, an overwhelming 97% of companies surveyed believe the veteran's strong sense of responsibility is their number one factor in hiring military.[3]

However, some companies have misperceptions about the risks and challenges associated with hiring employees with military experience. For example, the survey demonstrated in some cases a concern that former military employees need extra time to adapt to new workplace cultures. An option for you is to gravitate toward military friendly companies. The good news is that there are numerous military friendly companies, with specific hiring sites. Also be aware, big corporations such like Google, Chase, Amazon, and FedEx target veterans, providing resources and veteran support assistance. By knowing the environment and yourself, you can make quality decisions on potential future employers.

Consider these misperceptions as you interact with recruiters and hiring managers. Understand their concerns and plan your answers to interview questions accordingly. By arming yourself, you will relieve concerns and frustrations during your discussions. Remember, the skills you have obtained in the past will carry you through your transition.

Personal Characteristics

Character, derived from the word characteristic, refers to the essence of a person or thing. Character is the combination of traits and attributes that makes us different from one another, as shown in Figure 2.2. Understand your characteristics and how you can use these to add value for your future employer.

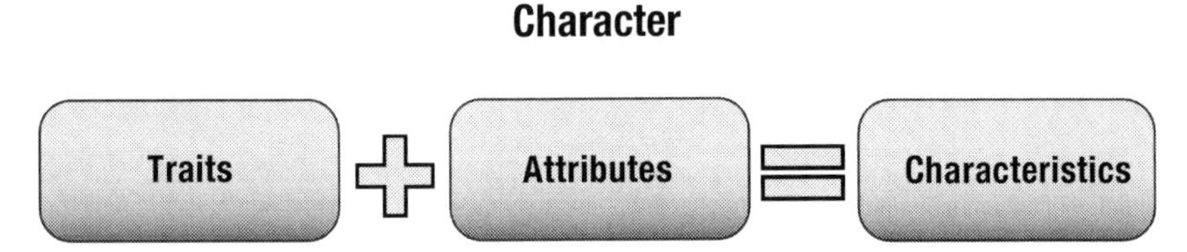

Figure 2.2 | Character

Traits are generally innate. A person may be outgoing or reclusive; shy or social. You likely still have some of the same personality traits that you were born with. Traits are often difficult to change. Attributes, as opposed to traits, are not ingrained. Attributes are learned over time and are based on external experiences. Attributes generally refer to a specific behavior or behaviors. Therefore, as a military service-member, you may have developed strong attributes during a challenging and difficult professional career or situation, such as combat or peace-keeping operation. Attributes such as motivation and enthusiasm are examples of characteristics that may change with your life or professional experience. A person may be committed or have strong integrity. He or she may be loyal or hard working. These attributes lead to certain behaviors, which can be strong predictors of how one will respond to different stimulus in the work environment.

Lesson learned from recent cyber issues in the public news highlighted six principles that should be part of the human factor in the cybersecurity profession: Integrity, depth of knowledge, procedural compliance, forceful backup, a questioning attitude, and formality in communication.[4]

Figure 2.3 | Six Cybersecurity Character Principles

While the specific skills sets in cybersecurity mentioned earlier are important, the foundation of the attitude and approach of the individual is just as critical. There have been a few formal studies of cybersecurity professionals, using psychological personality measures, and it is interesting to see that professionals in this field have some similar character traits with police officers.[4] Sarah Freed discovered in her research that cybersecurity professionals are a bit more cautious in trusting technology or people, since they are relied upon to protect systems and information, knowing what one person can secure given enough time, another may be able to circumvent. They are more adaptable to shifting situations, due to the nature of the job that requires agility to address cyber defense issues. They are logical, due to the technology in which they work, and assertive, as a result of the nature of the job to be protective.

From experience, those in the cybersecurity profession will also have developed a high level of curiosity, a deep desire to understand how something works. Combining with the cautious nature discussed above, the cybersecurity professional will always be testing the conditions, limits, and configurations established in order to find out any flaws. Since a cybersecurity professional will be most often charged with the protection of information assets, it is not unusual to see attributes where the individual takes on aspects of personal responsibility and ownership of a problem.

The cybersecurity profession is one that depends upon its workforce to behave ethically. In this book, ethics is defined as the science concerning the "right" and "wrong" of human action.[5] As such, members of the cybersecurity career field abide by a strict code of ethics and behavior, many following the code of ethics from organizations from which certifications are held. A great number of members of the military have already been exposed to and deeply understand ethical choices, and are intimately aware of the importance for owning and being responsible for their choices in life. Consequently, choosing an ethical course of action and doing the right thing, even in the face of opposition – regardless of the consequences – and actively encourage others to behave ethically, is a natural trait.

Those who come from the military also understand the importance of maintaining a professional presence. This is not necessarily just maintaining a professional appearance, though dressing appropriately for occupational and worksite requirements is expected; it is also the maturity of demonstrating self-control, of maintaining composure and keeping emotions in check while dealing calmly and effectively with stressful or difficult situations. It even includes the ability to accept criticism tactfully and attempt to learn from it.

Having served in the military, these attributes should not be new to you. You understand the need to accomplish the important aspects of our mission. You have learned what constitutes earning trust. You also realize that many depend upon our actions, whether it is our comrade-in-arms on the battlefield or our nation as a whole. You are answerable to others. In many instances you become as the author David Grossman described, "sheepdogs" defending the flock against the wolves.[6] You have had to learn to adapt and overcome obstacles, finding innovative and new ways to attack problems to ensure our mission.

Core Values

In addition to your attributes, you have been well indoctrinated into your services core values. Your time in the service has shaped you, through the installation of military core values, so use these to your advantage. Military core values are well understood and appreciated by employers. It is essential to understand how the military service has shaped you and your attributes. Whether you are Army, Navy, Air Force, Marine, or Coast Guard, you have valuable attributes that can be applied in the job market. Some veterans have managed people, computers, or weapon systems. The common desirable theme among former military is their core values (Figure 2.4).

Service	Core Values
Air Force	Integrity First, Service Before Self, Excellence In All We Do
Army	Loyalty, Duty, Respect, Selfless Service, Honor, Integrity, Personal Courage
Coast Guard	Honor, Respect, Devotion to Duty
Navy/Marines	Honor, Courage, Commitment

Figure 2.4 | Service Core Values

People hear the words *Loyalty, Duty, Respect, Selfless Service, Honor, Integrity, and Personal Courage* all the time. Service members learn these values during their initial training. For the rest of the time you spend in the military, you live these values every day in everything you do, 24 hours a day, seven days a week. These values are tremendous attributes. The question is: How do you relay these to the prospective employer? It is likely that employers consider hiring former service members because they believe they have these attributes. However, you will still need to demonstrate your *individual* traits and attributes. Knowing yourself is the first step in doing so.

In addition to your core values, your traditional military qualities such as professionalism, leadership, confidence, positive attitude, communications and organizational skills are all highly desired by commercial companies. Understanding your strengths and applying them to your job search and your career choice is key for your next job.

Your Undiscovered Corporate Skills

In addition to all of the previously mentioned characteristics and values, you should reflect and take note of your undiscovered skills. Left undiscovered, a prospective employer may fail to see desired skills.

Everyone is born with innate gifts and talents. Some of these you perform so easily that you hardly notice. Many of your finest qualities go unnoticed by yourself and others as shown in Figure 2.5. A reflective question here is: Have you taken the time to identify what you are naturally good at and where you excel? Are you a great communicator? Do you know how to push people to get a job done? How about motivating or mentoring others? This type of introspection will allow you to see what others observe and how you can capitalize on these abilities as you transition from the military.

Often, people overlook some very good non-work skills such as hobbies, travel, cars, etc. When looking to connect and establish rapor, many successes start with casual conversations on hobbies. Someone may be a great fisherman and feel that this is of no consequence in the work environment. They may have a

Undiscovered Skills
Understanding group dynamics
Ability to read the weather and predict storms
Always knowing and speaking the right words at the right moment
Knowing how to bring an individual back into the conversation
Understanding how to bring a group of people back into harmony
Loving the challenge of a puzzle
Motivating a group with low moral
Understanding group dynamics
Sensing direction, never lost

Figure 2.5 | Undiscovered Skills

tremendous understanding of when and where the fish will be biting. You may say, "Who cares about when and where the fish are schooling?" This can be parlayed into conversation openers to break the ice in meetings or customer engagements. This communication technique is commonly used with customers and sponsors. The best way to establish and gain consensus from stakeholders is by connecting with them on a personal level. The next time you go into the offices of a customer or hiring manager, look at the photos or items on the wall and try to figure out what this person is about. Inquire about something you see, positively and open-mindedly. You may very well find that you may have similar background or experiences. This is frequently how new relationships begin.

Do not underestimate any personal attribute that you have. Start with discovering what makes you unique and what defines you. List these out. Learn how they can assist you in the job market and at the office. Some of these qualities may be added at the top of your resume for personal attributes, which will be discussed later in the resume section of this chapter.

The bottom line is that you may have many traits, characteristics and attributes. These may be learned, innate, or yet undiscovered. Regardless, they are invaluable to you and your future employer and should be resume highlights. Recognize these features, understand their qualities in the workplace and try to apply them. Take the time now to reflect and learn how they can be of value to your future employer.

Why Are You a Desirable Employee?

Many of these core values and characteristics discussed are exactly what is desired of a quality cybersecurity professional. This is not a coincidence;

old-fashioned leadership is always essential. Arguably, some of the finest leaders in the world have been trained by the military. Forbes recently published the following reasons to hire veterans (Figure 2.6).

Quality	Description
Leadership	Platoon leader, group leader, team leader: military veterans work in a highly team-oriented and hierarchical environment. This means they know how to take orders – and when to give them.
Grace under pressure	If you're on the front lines in a war, you need to stay calm and function under extreme pressures. It makes some Human Resources HR and management calamities look trivial – after all what we do is HR/people management.
Performance and results-oriented	When you're in uniform you have a mission, one on which lives may be dependent. Performance and results are non-negotiable. You know how to get things done and you do them.
Self-sacrifice	Self-awareness and self-sacrifice. Leaders in the military have to watch out for their teams first and themselves second, which is a leadership scenario not always encountered in the Fortune 500.
Communication and goal-setting	Effective communicators build teams. Leaders set goals and teams accomplish them. You can't have one without the other.

Figure 2.6 | Five Reasons to Hire Veterans [7]

By virtue of military service, you already know how to track issues on a daily, if not hourly, basis. These types of organizational qualities are key for any successful cybersecurity manager. You have had to reassign tasks to other service members, take or give fitness tests, and oversee weapons cleaning; all simultaneously. It has been said that the difference between success and failure is based on whether you are highly organized or not. Are you?

Stress

You are battle hardened and have been through many experiences. Many of you have worked in very stressful and time sensitive environments, including combat zones. As you enter the job market, you will face other types of experiences. However, most civilians have not experienced the challenges that military lifestyle brings. Be confident about your ability to deal with difficult situations. The stress you have experienced is different and comes from wondering if the abandoned car beside the road is an improvised explosive device (IED). Stress is stress, but not all stress is the same and you have to develop a new understanding of stress in the commercial sector and confidently realize, "I've got this".

Preparing mentally to deal with stress during your transition is also essential. Stress will present itself during transition from home, work and seeking a new job. You need to work on your transitional responsibilities prior to your departure while the office will expect you to work. However, take the time to do the preparatory activities such as assembling a resume, branding and interview practicing. These activities, along with a potential family move with school age children can cause significant personal and marital stress. Finally, the job hunt can take its own toll with stress. Knowing how you cope with stress is very beneficial during the transitional period. For example, if you like to work out, stick with it. Take time for your stress reducing activities. It can make the difference between a smooth or painful transition.

Skills Translation

An understanding of how to translate and apply your skills to commercial cybersecurity is vital to your transition. You may perceive that you have little cybersecurity experience. But if you have been working within IT for any period of time, you have an understanding of cybersecurity skills and concepts. Cybersecurity surrounds all areas of IT; in fact, it has become so crucial to IT capabilities that cybersecurity has become its own career. Gaining an understanding of how your trained skills from your Navy Rating, Army Military Occupational Skill (MOS) and Air Force Specialty Code (AFSC) relate to the commercial cybersecurity occupations is essential. There are many formal military skills that are directly related to cybersecurity roles and responsibilities, such as the Air Force 3D0X3 - Cyber Surety AFSC, the Army 25D MOS - Cyber Network Defender, the Navy Information Dominance rate for Cryptologic Technician-Networks (CTN), and the Marine Corps 0689 MOS - Cybersecurity Technician. However, there are other military specialties that have exposure to the cybersecurity field, such as systems administrators, IT specialists, and information system technicians which have the foundational skills to move into the cybersecurity field as a civilian.

Understanding your background is the first step to identifying your developed skills from your occupation in the military. Given the breadth and impact cybersecurity has on IT, Figure 2.7 below presents the major technical IT and cybersecurity MOS, AFSC and Ratings with designators from the services. Items underlined within Figure 2.7 are skills directly related to cybersecurity. However, if you were not working in a cybersecurity career field in the military, do not be overly concerned. Most IT positions within the military have training and understanding of rudimentary cybersecurity concepts and are closely related to one or more of the cybersecurity functions. Therefore, by virtue of your military experience, with training, some additional education, and certification you may be well suited for a future career in cybersecurity.

Enlisted Cybersecurity & IT MOS, AFSC and Ratings

Army

17C Cyber Operations Specialist
25B Information technology specialist
25C Radio Operator / Maintainer
25D Cyber Network Defender
25F Network switching systems (OP-MAINT)
25L Cable systems installer-maintainer
25M Multimedia illustrator
25N Nodal network systems OP-MAINT
25P Microwave systems OP-MAINT
25Q Multichannel trans sys OP-MAINT
25S Satellite communication sys OP-MAINT
25U Signal support systems specialist
35T MI systems maintainer/integrator
94E Radio & Communications Security Repairer

Navy

AE Aviation Electrician
AT Aviation Electronics Technician
CTM Cryptologic Technician - Maintenance
CTN Cryptologic Technician - Networks
CTT Cryptologic Technician - Technical
CWE Cyber Warfare Engineering
ET Electronics Technician
IC Interior Communications Electrician
IT Information Systems Technician Surface
ITS Information Systems Technician Submarines
MC Mass Communication Specialist

Air Force

1B4 Cyberspace Defense Operations
2E1 Satellite, Wideband and Telemetry Systems
2E2 Network Infrastructure Systems
2E6 Communication Cable and Antenna Systems
3A0 Knowledge Operations Management
3C0 Communication-Computer Systems
3C1 Information Systems Technology
3D0X3 Cyber Security
3D0X4 Computer Systems Programming
3D1 IT and Client Systems

Marine Corps

0600 Basic Communications Marine
0612 Tactical Switching Operator
0613 Construction Wireman
0614 Unit Level Circuit Switch (ULCS) OP-MAINT
0618 Electronic Switching OP-MAINT
0627 SHF Satellite Communications OP-MAINT
0628 EHF Satellite Communications OP-MAINT
0648 Strategic Spectrum Manager
0651 Cyber Network Operator
0658 Tactical Data Network Gateway Sys Admin
0659 Cyber Network Systems Chief
0681 Information Security Technician
0689 Cyber Security Technician
0699 Communications Chief
2611 Cryptologic Digital Network Tech/Analyst
2651 Special Intel System Admin

Figure 2.7 | Enlisted Cybersecurity and IT MOSs, AFSCs and Ratings

Non-Commissioned Officers

Soldiers, Marines, Sailors and Airmen are trained how to perform specific IT duties after their initial training. As you were promoted to higher levels of responsibility as a Non-Commissioned Officer, you obtained considerable cross-functional IT, cybersecurity and leadership understanding.

Warrant Officers

As a group, Warrant Officers from the Army, Navy and Marine Corps are the most technically proficient service members in the military. Warrant Officers have the virtue of being a specialist in a specific technology area while regularly performing management functions across multiple IT fields. In general, Warrant Officers have had to manage sections, perform their individual specialty, while simultaneously educating and learning other IT or cybersecurity functions. Figure 2.8 depicts the IT and cybersecurity (underlined) occupations of the Warrant Officer Corps within the Army, Navy and Marine Corps.

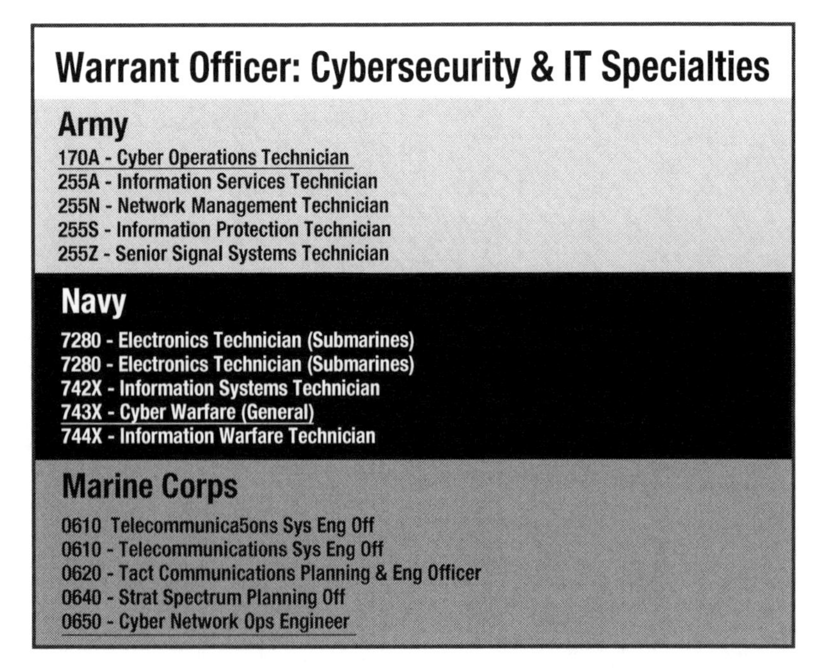

Figure 2.8 | Warrant Officer Cybersecurity and IT Specialties

Commissioned Officers

If you are a commissioned officer your career has probably taken on a management flavor for much of your military experience. The majority of officers are trained on a specific communication career field receiving some training in cybersecurity. Some take the time to personally develop their cybersecurity skills and become highly proficient. Many others take a generalized approach and educate themselves on aspects of IT and associated cybersecurity interoperability, leading to cybersecurity or IT management positions. Figure 2.9 below, depicts the basic branches and functional areas of commissioned officer's across the services within the IT and cybersecurity (underlined) career fields.

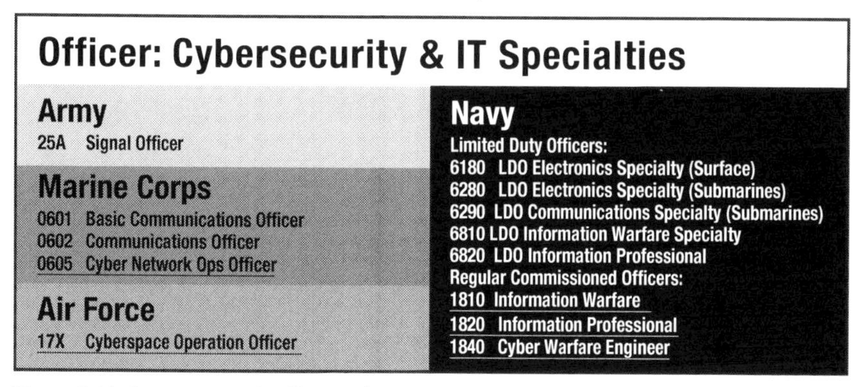

Figure 2.9 | Commissioned Officer Cybersecurity and IT Career Fields

Cybersecurity personnel are well versed in most IT functions, and most IT professionals are trained to maintain cybersecurity compliancy at the forefront of all performed tasks. Therefore, if you have an IT background in the military, your talents and knowledge will provide great dividends as you pursue a new career in cybersecurity. In fact, cybersecurity specialists are very knowledgeable in one or more IT functional areas.

With regard to NCO's, warrant and commissioned officers, seeking managerial positions after the military, the cybersecurity career field has managers. However, cybersecurity is a technical career field, and the best cybersecurity managers will have an extensive IT and cybersecurity background.

Remember, know yourself and consider your capabilities. With certification, education and experience, cybersecurity management may be a perfect professional goal to pursue.

Skill Translation Considerations

Workplace satisfaction considers how comfortable and satisfied you are with day-to-day efforts. Therefore, carefully consider such factors as the organization you work for, your job and the functions you will perform. In the commercial world, your military and IT skills relate to actual cybersecurity core functions (Figure 2.10). As you transition into a cybersecurity position, you will probably be performing one or more of these core functions. You may be familiar or already have experience working in a closely related function. Later, in Chapter 3, these cybersecurity core functions will be elaborated and you will be introduced to these cybersecurity specialty areas, occupations and a recommended method for obtaining the positions through preparation, education and certification. This unique and consolidated method allows for ease of understanding commercial cybersecurity during your transition.

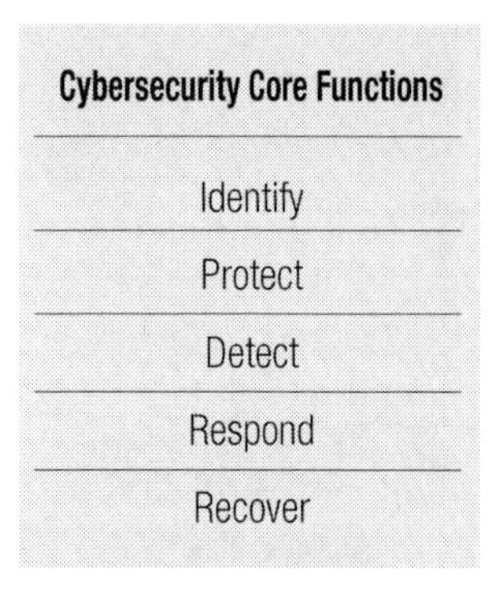

Figure 2.10
Cybersecurity Core Functions

There are a few considerations that could impact and influence your decision making process during your transition. Seek out the most appropriate position for yourself based on the amalgamation of your personality, desires and capabilities. Consider the following influences when analyzing your experiences as they relate to the cybersecurity core functions.

First, your ***skills may transcend many cybersecurity functions.*** Cybersecurity is woven into the fabric of all IT career fields in addition to having its own career field and positions. Many of your skills acquired during the service through your assignments have potentially fallen into multiple career fields or functions. Carefully consider what you enjoy doing and the function(s) that you think you desire the most.

Second, even though you were assigned a particular MOS, AFSC or rating while in the service, you may have performed considerable work within one of the other cybersecurity core functions or have had formal or cross training more closely aligned with one of the other IT functions.

Third, you may find that you have an affinity or desire to work performing a different cybersecurity core function as a civilian. You may desire to perform the study required in one or more functions that you found more enjoyable and will lead to a more personally appropriate initial post military career.

Translation take-away

Regardless of your experience in the service, thinking about your personal desires with regard to the cybersecurity core functions will improve your focus on how to build your resume, and where to seek employment. You need to be able to translate your experience. To assist with this translation, a further understanding of the functions and associated occupations are provided later in Chapter 3. Remember, you and your desires are unique and you must be able to relay your experiences to the commercial hiring manager.

Assessment #1 *(Personal Characteristics)*

This assessment explores your personal readiness and preparedness for transition. You may answer the assessment questions here. When you are ready to analyze them, refer to Chapter 5. You can also use the companion guide to this book, available for download and print out on-line at www.Gr8MilitaryCyber.com. Assessment #1 (Figure 2.11) requires you to analyze your personal characteristics, traits and abilities. Read each question and choose the best answer for you.

1: Personal Characteristics	Strongly Disagree	Disagree	Neither Agree OR Disagree	Agree	Strongly Agree
I enjoy working with and being around people in the IT career field.					
I easily apply my IT skills and referential knowledge when performing tasks.					
I tend to lead tasks when given the opportunity.					
I can perform well in a stressful environment.					
I adapt quickly to changing environments.					
I enjoy being part of a team effort.					
I have the ability to learn Information Technology concepts quickly.					
I enjoy working in IT and solving Information Technology problems.					
I have thoroughly analyzed the Technical/Management question with regard to my future career path.					
I proactively desire to learn and experience new IT concepts and trends.					

Figure 2.11 | Personal Characteristics

SWOT Analysis

As another tool for your transition preparation and ability to know yourself, the Strength, Weaknesses, Opportunities and Threats (SWOT) analysis is presented. SWOT analysis originally developed for strategy and marketing has been used extensively by business developers. SWOT is a method for determining competitive advantage in the market place. This tool can also be used to help determine your competitive advantage to the job market competition. Performing a self-analysis to determine your abilities or challenges within these four areas will not only give you a greater understanding of yourself, but provide a level of confidence you need to be competitive. Figure 2.12 depicts those characteristics or attributes common to military personnel based on their typical military experience.

Personal Environmental Factors

As you begin your transition it is important to understand your personal environmental factors. These factors affect you, your family, and your job opportunities. If you are like most, you will work after you transition from the military. If married, you certainly need to take into consideration your family's environmental requirements as you make decisions. Therefore, ensure you work through this section with them. If single, some of the considerations listed here may be relevant to your extended family or future plans.

Family and Health

As you transition, you need to consider your special family needs. Being close to extended family may constrain your job searching to certain geographic areas. Proximity to airports and hospitals might also require consideration.

There are many family issues to consider during your transition. Does your spouse need or want to work? Can they find jobs at the location you desire? Will he or she require more training or education? Will you or your family need to be near a university or college? Have you studied or discussed sharing your Post 911 G.I. Bill benefits with your family?

Strengths

Internal, positive aspects under your control to exploit:

- Military work experience (Ch. 2)
- Education (Ch. 3)
- Tech knowledge (Ch. 2)
- Transferable characteristics -communication, leadership, teamwork (Ch. 2)
- Personal attributes - ability to work under pressure, work ethic, etc. (Ch. 2)
- Innate Military Core Values (Ch. 2)
- Ability to assess and perform introspection on your capabilities (Ch. 5)
- Ability to gain certification (Ch. 3)

Weaknesses

Negative aspects you control and can improve upon:

- Lack of work experience (Ch. 3)
- Lack of understanding of job market (Ch. 3)
- Lack of commercial vernacular (Ch. 3)
- Negative self-image (Ch. 2)
- Negative misconceptions about former military (Ch. 2)
- Lack of professional or career IT/Cybersecurity knowledge (Ch. 3)

Opportunities

Positive, external conditions outside of your control that you can exploit:

- Growth in IT/Cybersecurity career field (Ch. 2)
- Military friendly companies (Ch. 2)
- Opportunities available through further educational and certification (Ch. 3)
- Fields in need of military attributes (Ch. 2)
- Opportunities available with greater preparation and self-knowledge (Ch. 3)
- Opportunities by greater understanding of commercial career field and market place (Ch. 4)
- Networking with seasoned IT Professionals (Ch.3)

Threats

Negative, external conditions you cannot control, but can reduce the effect:

- Knowing your competition (Ch. 3)
- Negative misconceptions about former military (Ch. 2)
- Competitors with better job hunting capabilities (Ch. 2)
- Obstacles - lack of education and certification (Ch. 3)
- Competitors with superior skills (Ch. 3)
- Failure to stay marketable (Ch.3)

Figure 2.12 | SWOT Analysis

A few questions you should consider are:

- Do you have access to medical care or a veterans Administration hospital?
- Do you understand the impact on you and your family with regard to the loss of military benefits?
- Do you know how much risk you and your family are willing to take with your next position?

> "*...success is to be measured not so much by the position that one has reached in life, as by the obstacles which he has had to overcome while trying to succeed.*"
>
> ~ Booker T. Washington

Work- Life Balance

Another environmental factor to take into consideration as you transition is your work life balance. You have worked hard in the military. Part of the assessment process is understanding where you reside on the work-life balance continuum. When looking for a job you should consider work-life attributes such as the demands that your occupation will require. Are you ready to climb the corporate ladder? You may find a demanding job and make a lot of money; but is that what you want for your retirement job? Occasionally, you can find a job with great work-life balance and make lots of money. In general however, if you make $120K, you should generally expect to put forth a $120 K effort.

One of the occupational hazards in cybersecurity is a progressive loss of WLB (Figure 2.13). Your personal investment in cyber knowledge and experience will allow you to achieve greater expertise, accomplishment, fulfillment and financial reward. It is easy to be caught up in the cycle of hard work and reward. Be cautious, as a successful career must have balance or one will burn out personally, professionally, or both.

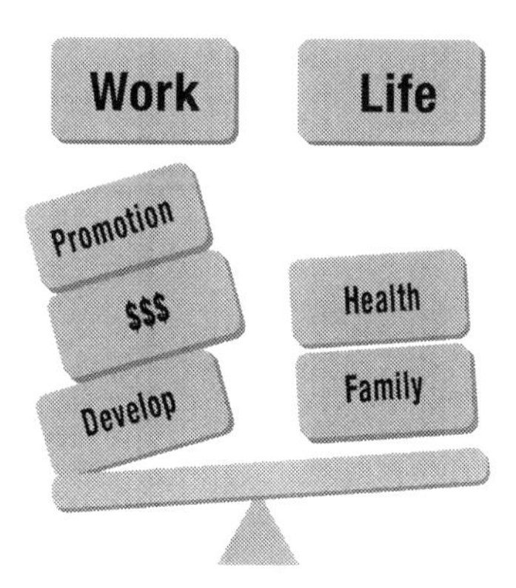

Figure 2.13 | Work-Life Balance

Location

Location, Location, Location! - A phrase we are all quite familiar with. A critical consideration is moving to the location of your choice prior to your transition. It can be challenging and very expensive to get back to your U.S. home or to your desired location on your own dime, especially if overseas. You can save a tremendous amount of money if you can have the military move you back to your home of record, or if you can take your last assignment at your desired location. Another advantage to making this happen as part of your transition or retirement would be the ability to begin building your future local network early. If you know where you are going to end up, begin building your network remotely. Here are a few other questions you should ask yourself if you have not already:

- Have you considered the location of your next job?
- Have you looked at the climate as it relates to your health, hobbies and personal activities?
- What is the unemployment rate?
- How many government related jobs exist in the local area?
- What is the cost of living?
- Do you have the need or desire to be near a military base so you can use the commissary, exchange and other facilities?
- Are you looking for a rural or urban life experience?
- Do you wish to live overseas?

Assessment #2 *(Environmental Factors)*

The goal of the second assessment, presented in Figure 2.14, is for you to perform a personal analysis of the associated environmental issues with your transition. As with the first assessment, read each question and choose the best answer. Refer to Chapter 5 when you are ready to analyze the results.

2: Environmental Factors	Strongly Disagree	Disagree	Neither Agree OR Disagree	Agree	Strongly Agree
I have performed a post-military financial analysis, to include the loss of military benefits if applicable.					
I have determined my desired geographic location with regard to such factors as healthy lifestyle, allergies, health care access, hobbies, weather and entertainment.					
I have considered my family's special needs in my transition planning.					
I have analyzed and understand myself with regard to work life balance.					
I have given thought to my future location with regard to military base and/or VA Hospital proximity.					
I have studied transition locations with regard to extended family and transportation hub.					
I have analyzed my transition location with regard to future employment, taxation, real estate cost, and overall cost of living.					
I have considered my spouses occupation and their ability to find work.					
I have taken into account my children's primary, secondary and/or college education requirements.					
My family is supportive of my transition into another career.					

Figure 2.14 | Environmental Factors Assessment

Timing

As the saying goes "Timing is everything." As in any transition, timing is a key factor. Are you ready to leave? Do you have to leave? Are you satisfied with your military efforts and are ready to move on? These questions are mixed to ascertain your level of readiness to transition from the service. With regard to your timing, this section includes an analysis of many elements, such as studying the educational benefits, developing and refining your resume, making interview preparations, and approaching certification in the cybersecurity field.

The following timing-related topics are presented as rhetorical questions for your comprehension, personal review and self-organization.

Is the Timing Right?

Are you ready to go? You do not want to regret your transition, as there is no going back if you still have something left to do in the military. There are many things to consider about timing. Gut instinct is probably not the best method for this determination. Looking at the associated timing issues and conducting self-assessments will likely provide a better result. These decisions should be made with a clear head and strong conviction. You may not be able to choose when to leave the service, but you can choose to prepare yourself as best as possible. The bottom line – prepare with the limited time you have. Below are some things to consider when deciding if the timing is right to leave the service.

Are You Having Fun?

This may sound silly, but are you having fun in the military? Only you can determine if you are enjoying active duty. In general, active duty personnel truly enjoy the military lifestyle and the associated excitement. Many people look back at their time in service and remember their experience fondly. Others look back on their military service as an accumulation of tough days. However, you should expect to have tough days in your commercial job. Some will remark, "Wow, did I do the right thing getting out?" Just remember, the grass is not always greener on the other side.

Have You Achieved Your Personal Goals for Military Service?

Achieving your personal goals in the military can be quite challenging, especially in today's world. You may have specific goals you were trying to obtain that are no longer attainable. You may also have a brilliant career ahead of you. Making the decision to get out of the service is always difficult. If you have accomplished your primary goals and objectives for military service, there is no need to fret about whether you should stay any longer. You may be painfully aware that you have obtained the highest rank possible. Remember, everyone gets passed over for promotion at some point. Congress continually adjusts the size of the military based on the needs of the nation and the defense budget. The services have had to reduce their end-strengths in the past, are doing it now, and will do so again in the future. Everyone undergoes assessment and some will be involuntarily released from active duty. If this is your situation, be prepared and transition in a positive manner.

Has A Good Transitional Job Opportunity Presented Itself?

Many veterans have stepped out of the service straight into great jobs. This occurs with some degree of frequency, but it is not the norm. Often your first job is "transitional". After being out a while, you realize that your first job is probably not the one you desire. Remember, it is ok to test the waters when you first get out. Regardless, if you desire to grow and develop you may have to move on.

Not everyone will have a job in his or her back pocket when transitioning. The question that you should ask yourself is "Am I taking all the appropriate steps for a job opportunity to present itself when ready?"

Occupation or Vocation?

One of the many challenges that you will face during transition is the vexing decision of paying bills or pursuing your dreams. You will probably spend considerable time thinking about enabling uninterrupted cash flow, the best company to pursue and what location to settle. Reflection, analysis and alignment of your life's work will be pushed to another day, never enabling full personal passion.

Todd Henry explains in his book "Die Empty", the graveyard is the most valuable land in the world. Buried, here lay all the unwritten novels, un-launched business and all the things that were to be accomplished tomorrow.[8]

> ***"When opportunity comes, it's too late to prepare."***
>
> ~ John Wooden

Bottom line, many of us have yet to discern the difference between our occupation and our vocation. You may not find contentment in your occupational tasks, as you probably will not be fulfilling your dreams and you will be continually frustrated.[9] It takes time and reflection to discern your life's work. "Our occupation is how we make a living… Our vocation, on the other hand, is what we're inherently wired for. It's less likely to consist of a set of tasks and more likely to consist of a set of themes."[10] Tremendous satisfaction is found when making a living while pursuing your life's work.

Got Education? Certification?

Can you list your skills and education? Are you comfortable with this list? Do you want or feel the need to acquire more? The company that hires you does not always provide skills and education training at the onset. You must be ready to step in and work. Organizations occasionally offer training; however, you may need to sign an agreement to pay back the training fees or commit to an additional time period. The military is a great environment for training and learning because of all the educational programs and opportunities available. Every branch of service offers some form of military tuition assistance while on active duty. This lucrative benefit goes away upon transition and should be used prior to your departure from the service. Further, you may be able to get the service to pay for specialized IT related certification training before departing. Each service has on-line guidance for credentialing and certification. Pursue these avenues with a great vengeance before departing service.

Shortly after your transition from the service, you should obtain a Post 911 G.I. Bill certificate of eligibility from the Veteran's Administration. This is the essential starting point for using this tremendous educational benefit for you and perhaps your family's education. You may be eligible for this VA-administered program, if you have at least 90 days of aggregate active duty service after September 10, 2001, and are honorably discharged or were discharged with a service-connected disability.[11]

How is Your Financial Readiness?

Have you saved enough to survive the transition? These dollars need to be in short term savings and not locked up in a retirement account, to avoid penalties. For many, the question is, "How much should you keep in a 'rainy-day' fund?" According to the Bureau of Labor Statistics, an acceptable measure of three to six months' worth of expenses may no longer apply. "A lot of experts now recommend that everyone keep nine months to one year of income in an emergency account in case of job loss," says Gail Cunningham, spokeswoman for the National Foundation for Credit Counseling in Washington, D.C.[12]

Have You Prepared Your Resume?

There is a tremendous amount of information available to assist military veterans in the preparation of their resumes. This book is not intended to be a definitive guide on resume building. Discussions on how to enhance and communicate your brand and how to avoid common resume "landmines" or pitfalls frequently encountered by your fellow service members are provided. Remember, a powerful, impactful, well-written resume using commercial and business language, combined with the right format and branding power, can set you apart and propel you to a rewarding position in the private sector. Your resume and cover letters are your personal calling cards.[13] To create a well-branded and powerful resume you will need to go beyond providing your job description.

Be aware that commercial and civil service resumes can be very different. A few years ago, it was best practice to create a special resume with a specific format when applying for civil service positions. However, with the development of USAJOBS.gov, you can upload your resume to this website and no longer use a resume builder for civil service jobs.

Your Military Experience is Unique!

Many transitioning service members have challenges talking about the uniqueness of the military experience with civilian hiring managers. You must capitalize on the extraordinary capabilities that you have achieved while in the service. You will need to speak to the value and difference you made while serving in each position. Capture the size, quantity of personnel and possible multiple geographic locations that you had to coordinate or synchronize in each position. You will need to talk about the impact and volume of what you handled on a daily basis.

Resume Writing: Art and Science

There is a definite skill to writing a resume. It is an art to speak about yourself and connect your value to the value desired by a company. It is a science to include the key terms in your resume so a robot search engine can identify those words within your resume and put it at the top of their pile for consideration. There are many tools and books to assist you with this.

> *"Be bold. Most of us have a sense of humility, but a resume isn't the place for it."*
>
> ~ Anonymous

You will need to write and re-write your resume. Use your personal network smartly. For example, if you are searching for a civil servant position connect with military friends or colleagues that have made that transition. Use other networking groups from professional or other non-military organizations for commercial insight and guidance. You will need to modify the resume until you are comfortable with it. If you are challenged with resume writing and have money for professional preparation, this may be a good investment.

It is recommended to post your resume on hiring sites like Monster.com, Indeed.com, and CareerBuilder.com. These sites are scanned on a regular basis and you will get frequent emails informing you of opportunities. Even if the job is not exactly what you desire, apply. If you get an interview, pursue it and get a feel for the company and its opportunity, as it might be better than originally understood.

Resume Format

Impact! When your resume gets in front of a recruiter or hiring manager, it has only around twelve seconds to do its job. It needs to be clear and error-free and most importantly, show your value! The three major formats presenting their particular value are listed in Figure 2.15, below:

Resume Type	Description
Chronological	Starts by listing your work history, with the most recent position listed first. Jobs are listed in reverse chronological order – with current, or most recent job, first. Employers typically prefer chronological, easy to see jobs held and when worked. Works well for job seekers with strong, solid work history.
Functional	Focuses on your skills and experience, rather than on your chronological work history. Used most often for changing careers or gaps in employment history.
Combination (Hybrid)	Lists skills and experience first. Employment history is listed next. Highlights relevant skills to the job you are applying for, while providing chronological work history that employers prefer.

Figure 2.15 | Resume Types[14]

Employers tend to favor a resume that is easy to follow and clearly communicates your professional track. If you plan on writing your own and have 10 or more years of experience and education, select a format that concentrates on your assignments, your accomplishments (value), and education. A great guide for specific resume examples and templates can be found in the book "*The Military to Civilian Transition Guide: Secrets to Finding Great Jobs and Employers.*"[15]

Common Resume Pitfalls

The following errors in resume writing are often found in service member resumes as they prepare for transition. Avoiding these problem areas will increase the probability of your resume getting through the human resource staff screening and into the hands of the hiring official.

Resume is written in Service Member Jargon

Examples include such terms as command and control, tactics, ISR, execution of battle plans, OPTEMPO, weaponry. There is no place for military jargon or vernacular in your commerical resume. Unit names are typically not significant. Write your resume with your audience in mind. Most of the people scanning it are human resources professionals who understand their industry and recruiting, not mortar ranges and targeting of terrorist networks. Focus on plain business language and your potential value to an employer. Remember, many years of military service and the word "retired" may arouse undesirable assumptions.

Very Long Resume

A resume should be two pages or less in length. Do not try to cram 25+ years of military service into the resume. Instead, adjust your format and focus on your last 10-12 years. Employers will thank for you for this.

Resume with No Direction

"Operations Manager, Sales Manager, Director of Business Planning and jack of all trades." Do not let your resume display uncertainty or ambiguous career goals. Your resume should not float between work experience narratives with no central focus. You need to make a decision and decide what you want to place in your objective statement and write your resume to that. You can always change your mind with the next version of your resume or have multiple resumes, but you have to focus on one career direction per resume. Remember, you are telling a story and creating a brand for yourself. Your resume must show direction and tell your personal story as it relates to the position for which you are applying.

> ***"Be so good they can't ignore you."***
>
> ~ Steve Martin

Job Duties Only

Often, a service member's first cut on a resume focuses on the job duties performed. This makes sense as these are easily transferred from your military evaluations. However this technique does not work. Remember: you are your own best salesman! You need to focus on achievements and the impact you made to show value and worth to your potential employer. By only listing job duties, you are telling a prospective employer you do not bring much to the table other than following direction. If you lack education, make sure to highlight your professional development and your certifications.

Your resume needs to show how you can help provide value from the prospective company's perspective in the form of cybersecurity success, strategy, financial goals, market penetration, or process improvement. Demonstrate you are more than an employee and that you are an asset to any team. Believe it or not, everyone else competing for that same job knows this secret!

Getting to the Top

How do you stand out? Getting your resume to the top of a hiring managers list among hundreds of candidates will be challenging. You obviously want your resume to be noteworthy, but you do not want to appear arrogant or inexperienced. You must be understood by hiring managers, which can be a difficult task for anyone in transition. Here are a few pointers:

Customize for the Intended Audience

As you transition, you must be flexible and versatile. Make sure your resume is appropriate, as every company and position is different. Therefore, you may need several different versions of your resume; each emphasizing different facets of your career objectives and achievements. Be consistent and do not contradict yourself.

Get to the Point

Consider integrating the specific job posting title into your objective statement. Don't present a high level, generalized and vague comment about how you are looking for a challenging position with a dynamic company as an accomplished professional. Describe your pertinent experiences and qualifications in quick and energetic terms.

> ***"Be yourself, everyone else is already taken."***
>
> ~ Oscar Wilde

Don't Over Embellish, but Tell a Great Story

Recruiters expect a resume to reflect an element of spin, but over exaggeration will get you in trouble every time. Place the most favorable light on yourself and your achievements. However, excessive embellishments may keep you from getting hired and nothing is more miserable than being placed in a position where you are underqualified and cannot perform well.

Integrate Keywords from the Job Posting

Today, keyword search is a screening criterion. Don't overdo it, but ensure sure keywords are present in your resume. This is critical for all online applications and resumes, as most are screened by computer searches. Further, you will receive subsequent contact for positions that you have not applied for. Do you satisfy the criteria on the job posting? If so, do you reflect that on your resume? Get the keywords on your resume.

Avoid "en vogue" Terms and Words

Your resume should not read as if has been pulled from the latest business magazine or thesaurus. Forget over-used words and phrases; try to be original. However, don't overuse big words when simplistic language will do.

Remember, there are no mind tricks to influence your selection by a human resources recruiter. Sending out resumes is a matter of trial and error. You will have to keep submitting and experimenting with different formats and approaches until something works for you. With ingenuity and realistic expectations, you will create a bulletproof resume that represents well and lands you a great job.[16]

Professional Branding

You are a professional brand. You might not necessarily realize this fact when you begin your transition, but it is true. Your resume, LinkedIn® profile, and job applications should all mutually support your common brand. Focus on key items like leadership or a subject matter expertise. Build a brand foundation that resonates throughout the resume. It is important to ensure your professional experience and education reflects who you are. Prospective hiring officials should have no doubt on your level of expertise and what you bring to the table. Make sure your Facebook and LinkedIn pages are strictly professional, as hiring professionals look at them.

Achievements

Focus on both your achievements and career history, while highlighting your measurable capabilities and impact on the organization by personifying and enhancing your professional brand. A two-page resume should contain enough power when written well. You must show the impact you made on all previous positions. Listing that you had a job without any impact will not get you hired. Remember, they are hiring you and what you can bring to the table.

Cover Letter – Icing on the Cake

Experts in the placement field say that the well-written cover letter, not the resume, will land more job interviews. As a transitioning service member, it would be a tragic mistake not to spend the time and effort necessary for a personalized cover letter, each time you submit an application. So the question is can you rapidly construct a great cover letter? Here is some advice for constructing a great cover letter.

> ***"The resume focuses on you and the past. The cover letter focuses on the employer and the future..."***
>
> ~ Joyce Lain Kennedy, *Cover Letters for Dummies*

Be Brief

A short, pithy, excited and to the point cover letter will get your cover letter read. Human resources and hiring managers are not going to read through a long boring document, when they are quickly scanning for the right candidate. Often times, less is more.

Layout

Remember to address your cover letter to someone! Find out who will receive the cover letter and address your cover letter to them. If you cannot get this information, open with a subject line like: "Cover Letter: Your Name, Your Credential". Open the cover letter with a hook. The first sentence must grip the reader and will almost guarantee your cover letter and resume get a much closer look. You can do this through one of several methods.

- **Excitement** - You can express your excitement for the job opportunity. This translates to motivation and dedication. This can make HR want to find out more about your qualifications.

- **Using keywords** - Knowing that scanning or applicant tracking systems are widely used, another approach to the opening line is to make it key-word-heavy.

- **Name dropping** - Using a connection is foreign concept to many service members, because we don't do this in the military. If someone in your professional network refers you, don't hesitate to drop the name, straight away. This is done all the time in the commercial world and people often receive referral dollars for doing so. Remember, time is money and this method helps HR rapidly fill positions with quality candidates.
- **Current event** - Your cover letter opener can impact employers by demonstrating your knowledge of recent news associated with the company and relay that to the position you are applying for. Let them know why you would be the best candidate as relative to this news.

Make sure your cover letter communicates what you can do for the business, how you will benefit the company and its bottom line. You may need to take a few minutes and perform some internet searches to relate your added value in clear terms.

Ensure you have an enthusiastic ending and request something. Ask the employer for some kind of action. Go ahead and request an opportunity to interview this week or earliest convenience. Thank them for the opportunity. Your closing should assume you are going to land the interview.

T&T - Transportable & Tailorable

You want to be able to rapidly reuse your cover letter over and over again. So you need to create a folder for cover letters. You need to be able to quickly tailor the opening and cover letter to relate your skills to the essential elements of the job announcement. Don't forget to save your cover letter for quick modification and future use.

Remember, the cover letter is your marketing sheet. There only purpose for the cover letter is to get job interviews. The more interviews you attend, the wider range of opportunities you will receive. Remember, applying and interviewing for jobs is a career long process and it takes lots of practice.

Got Interviews?

> ***I AM…***
> ***Two of the most powerful words. For what you put after them shapes your reality.***
>
> ~ Anonymous

Practicing interviewing is absolutely essential. Interviewing is like fishing - you need to practice. If a resume is your bait and hook, use the interview to reel them in. Seek out and go on interviews regularly just to stay in practice. Interviewing is a very special skill. It takes a lot of time and finesse to be able to figure out the appropriate responses to the questions that your future employers are asking. Additionally, always be prepared to ask the hiring supervisor questions as well. This is a good indicator that you have done your homework and are showing an interest in what they do. Ensure you have studied the position description and company before the interview, so you can ask clarifying questions and gain more insight. Be honest during the interview. Do not overstate your capabilities. If you find you are not selected, you can and should ask why. If you make a mistake, you want to know so you can keep from making the same mistake again. Remember the adage, practice makes perfect. You can always inquire on other opportunities they know of within or outside their unit.[17]

Can You Communicate Your Characteristics to the Hiring Manager?

Communication is critical when dealing with a hiring manager. Normally, you will only get a few minutes with them. Most will sum up an applicant within the first five minutes. This is the opportunity to tell them what is not on the resume. Let them know you are the best candidate for the job. Huge dividends will be paid to the candidate who, prior to the interview, learns all they can about the company and its operations, their future supervisor, and the hiring manager.

After you have written your resume and find yourself in an interview, make sure you approach with enthusiasm. Interlace discussions of your skills, flexibility, military traits, passion and trustworthiness to the hiring manager. Use personal experiences resulting in positive end-states. Always communicate your best characteristics reflecting the attributes you have. It is time to unfold your story with enthusiasm and relevance to the company. Hiring managers view this positively.

Finally, unless specifically asked, never speak about your shortfalls. However, be prepared to answer the question, "Tell us about a time you failed". These are great opportunities to explain challenges that you have experienced. It is not about the change or failure that happened, it is how and what you did after to carry on and learn from it. What is important is to show how you turned the situation around for the good and future results. You need a great answer in your hip pocket that indicates you learned from the experience.

Have you Developed a Network?

You might think this would be natural expectation in a cybersecurity book, but in this case the "network" is a human one. Networking (or marketing) yourself is all about establishing positive relationships with people. Networking is about a "win-win" dynamic, so you don't want to make any of the relationships only about you. Actively involving yourself in networking opportunities provides insight into the market and current events. Developing your network is a two-pronged attack. One must have a local network and a virtual network. A great way to develop local networks is to volunteer at your local military association such as the Navy League, Association of the United States Army, Air Force Association, or Marine Corps Association. Professional organizations that include both government and private industry are also great networking opportunities, such as the Armed Forces Communications and Electronics Association (AFCEA) and the Cybersecurity Nexus (CSX) at the Information Systems Audit and Control Association, now known simply as ISACA. There are also professional certification and training organizations, such as the International Information Systems Security Certification Consortium or (ISC)2, the American Society of Industrial Security (ASIS), and the Project Management Institute (PMI).

Each of these organizations (Figure 2.16) have local chapters around the country and potentially in your local area. These organizations and associations not only offer national meetings, but often will have regional and local chapter meetings. Each one of these groups actively seeks volunteers. Volunteer and you will not only grow in your understanding of commercial cybersecurity; you will also be actively increasing your network.

ISACA® (formerly the Information Systems Audit and Control Association) **www.isaca.org/**	As an independent, nonprofit, global association, ISACA® engages in the development, adoption and use of globally accepted, industry-leading knowledge and practices for information systems.
International Information System Security Certification Consortium, Inc., (ISC)2® **www.isc2.org/**	(ISC)2® is the global, not-for-profit leader in educating and certifying information security professionals throughout their careers. (ISC)2® provides vendor-neutral education products, career services, and Gold Standard credentials to professionals in more than 160 countries
ASIS International (formerly the American Society for Industrial Security) **www.asisonline.org/**	ASIS International is a global community of security practitioners, each of whom has a role in the protection of assets - people, property, and/or information. ASIS members represent virtually every industry in the public and private sectors, and organizations of all sizes. From entry-level managers to CSOs to CEOs, from security veterans to consultants and those transitioning from law enforcement or the military, the ASIS community is global and diverse.
Armed Forces Communications and Electronics Association **www.afcea.org/**	AFCEA is an international organization that serves its members by providing a forum for the ethical exchange of information. AFCEA is dedicated to increasing knowledge through the exploration of issues relevant to its members in IT, communications, and electronics for the defense, homeland security and intelligence communities."

Figure 2.16 | Cybersecurity Organizations

It is a great concept as more and more folks join LinkedIn. The bottom line is that you need to network. It will pay huge dividends as you depart the service. Don't forget to start early.

Remember that people gravitate to people they like. When participating in any of these networking opportunities, take the time to say "thank you" to those that help you…and in turn, be willing to provide that same help and insight to others as you progress in your career. If you aren't asking how you can help you're missing out on opportunities.

Transition Assistance Program

Finally, have you attended your local transition assistance program? These programs are absolutely essential for teaching you the basics needed for a successful transition. Transition information and counseling for pre-separation, employment assistance, relocation, education and training, health and life insurance, finances, reserve affiliation, disabled veterans, and retirement are provided. However, you cannot expect to find a job from this program.

Military Transition Web Sites:

Air Force:
afpc.af.mil/lifeandcareer/transition.asp

Army:
acap.army.mil

Navy:
cnic.navy.mil/ffr/family_readiness/flee_and_family_support_program/transition_assistance.html

Marines:
mccscp.com/transition-assistance veterans-benefits

Coast Guard:
uscg.mil/hr/cg111/transition_assistance.asp

Assessment #3 *(Timing)*

In assessment #3 (Figure 2.17), you will look at personal preparedness and timing of your transition. As before, read each question and choose the best answer.

3: Timing	Strongly Disagree	Disagree	Neither Agree OR Disagree	Agree	Strongly Agree
I am ready to leave the military experience behind.					
I have met my career goals for the military.					
I am enjoying or looking forward to making plans for my military transition.					
My resume has been completed and reviewed by a civilian professional.					
I have established a network of professionals in and out of the service.					
I have saved several months salary for financial sustainment during transition.					
I have successfully attended a local military transition assistance program.					
I have successfully branded myself on LinkedIn, Facebook or with appropriate professional associations.					
I have practiced my interviewing skills.					
I have looking forward to departing the service.					

Figure 2.17 | Timing Assessment

Knowing yourself is critical when competing in today's job market. Seek professional enhancement at every turn. Do not be afraid to reach out to new opportunities and analyze alternative paths. Try different angles and exploit those areas where you get traction. The story below depicts one young woman who, though she didn't transition directly from the military, found that regardless of one's current job, building upon the strengths of your background, if you actively pursue the opportunities available you can end up successfully transitioning out of one field and end up working in the cybersecurity field today.

Steve Corcoran
Building on a Transitional Challenge

GROWING UP IN NEW JERSEY, STEVE CORCORAN ENJOYED SCHOOL AND EXCELLED IN SPORTS. He always wanted adventure, constantly searching for something different and "Outside". When materialization of that dream began to look bleak, he set his eyes on the Marine Corps.

Steve attended and graduated from William Paterson University in 1985, commissioning as a Second Lieutenant in the U.S. Marine Corps two weeks later. In a highly successful career that lasted 28 years, Steve contributed to virtually every major combat operation and humanitarian operation during that time frame to include Panama, South West Asia, the Balkans, Somalia, Iraq, Afghanistan and Horn of Africa. He commanded at every level from Lieutenant through Colonel, performed as a Staff Officer at every level of the Marine Air Ground task Force, numerous times at Joint Task Forces and Joint Special Operations Task Forces as well as at United States Central Command where he was assigned as Chief of Operations and Plans for the J6 Directorate, supporting Operation Iraqi Freedom and Operation Enduring Freedom.

For the last eight years of his career, Steve was immersed in cybersecurity operations with the military, thus validating his transition into the cybersecurity career field a natural progression.

Colonel Steve Corcoran's culminating assignment was Command of the Joint Communications Support Element (Airborne), supporting operations in support of Special Operations and Conventional Operations, world-wide. With the war effort and his love of the command he served, he lost track of his transition. He retired with almost no preparation but was optimistic because he was confident in his abilities and always landed with the best organizations and units. He desired to pursue the commercial market place and try something completely different.

Steve took a job working for a company that recruited him and saw his talent, but also desired to have him leverage his personal contacts. Within a few weeks, Steve was being asked to do things that he did not feel comfortable with, ethically. After a few more days, his conscience would not allow him to work for this organization any longer and he left unceremoniously; feeling so strongly about his assessment of the firm, he returned the compensation that he had previously earned.

Humbled, and a bit taken aback by his failure to see what was unfolding in front of him, Steve had no job, had performed no preparation prior to leaving the service other than medical and dental and was struggling to figure out his next move. He reflected upon his career and decided to "go to ground". He began to put together a plan, incorporating his Marine Core values and training. To not fall into a similar trap, Steve developed the following credo for his job search:

- *He must believe in what his company does and how they do it to include a strong belief in the senior leaders.*
- *He will not work for a company leveraged by venture capital; those companies will mortgage tomorrow to pay for today.*
- *He will not work for a rolodex company because they use you for your contacts until you are no longer of value; and there is no concern for you and your relationships.*

As Steve began the real homework required for his military transition, he performed an "Intelligence Preparation of the Battlefield (IPB)" where he studied each company's reputation, goals, financials, leadership, age, team -mates and competitors. Once he knew the companies he wanted to purse he began to put together a network and communication plan to pursue those organizations.

Today Steve proudly states that the preparation and vetting that he conducted landed him with the best company in the world and he has no desire to work for another company. He is the Director of Cyber Strategy for the Telos Corporation, where he assists the DoD and the Intelligence Community in developing and implementing full spectrum cyber capabilities and specialized mission applications.

In summation, Steve believes that a transitioning veteran brings some valuable experience to a civilian organization. He believes that adverse and uncertain environments in which you served in the military, have prepared you for new challenges. The key is to understand that you are entering into a talent rich environment and even though you don't understand the totality of the business, your peers and leaders deserve the same respect that you afforded the same while on active duty.

3

Cybersecurity Profession Basics

CYBERSECURITY IS MORE THAN JUST THE "TECHNOLOGY". Anyone really interested in getting into the cybersecurity profession already understands that there will be some technical knowledge required. However, there are also other related skill-sets that should be developed to be successful. In this chapter, we will examine the various job options or pathways presently available. Remembering that Moore's Law[1] said computer processing power doubles every two years, we can apply this logic to the cybersecurity industry and say with confidence that the specific skills one would need will most assuredly not remain static.

> *"If we continue to develop our technology without wisdom or prudence, our servant may prove to be our executioner."*
>
> ~ General Omar Bradley

In Chapter 2 you took stock and evaluated your general skills and abilities. You were asked to assess some of the cybersecurity responsibilities that were of interest. We also described some character traits that will help in this career field, since it is not just the training and education in the field that makes one successful.

In Chapter 3, you will take knowledge gained earlier in the book and combine it with a deeper understanding of the career field. As George Santayana wrote in *The Life of Reason*, 1905, "Those who cannot remember the past are condemned to repeat it"; therefore, we present a short history to gain an understanding on how the profession evolved. Specific professional knowledge and skills that are vital to success within the career field of cybersecurity are presented. Frameworks for the profession are offered to provide an understanding of the cybersecurity career field. Subsequently, specialty areas and the associated occupations are presented for your personal appraisal. Finally, associated certification and education for your successful entry into this career field are given.

Keep in mind that cybersecurity, as a specific discipline and profession, is in constant growth. The cybersecurity training site, Cybrary IT, reported the results of their Oct-Dec 2015 survey of 435 senior level technology and security professionals on the topic of cybersecurity job trends. They found that the demand for cybersecurity professionals is growing 4-times faster than the overall IT market, and 12-times faster than the total labor market. At the time of their survey, the participants reported more than a million open jobs in the cybersecurity profession, with 47% of companies planning to hire between 1 to 10 cybersecurity positions in 2016.[2]

We will explore some terms and names, since we have to be able to speak the language. It will be part of a history lesson, but it shows how dynamic the field is becoming. We will naturally discuss the specific work functions and general roles of cybersecurity, and then we will also look at training, education, and certifications one needs to be considered for a cybersecurity position.

History

Cybersecurity, cyberspace operations, and cyber are relatively new careers. However, we have had computers in government, academia, and business since the late 1940s. It is only in the past 40 years that cybersecurity or as it was called in various phases: information system security, computer security, and information assurance, was addressed. There were some specific transformations in the development and construction of computers which made them more common in industry and eventually put them in our homes, as well as in our pockets. This proliferation eventually drove us to protect them. Computer hardware has evolved so far through four major stages: vacuum tubes in the 1940s and 1950s, transistors in the 1950s and 1960s, integrated circuits in the 1960s and 1970s, and silicon chips in the 1970s to present day.

The ease of use has also evolved over time when only the most specialized scientists could use a computer in the 1950s, to when highly trained people could program and use computers in the 1960s and 1970s, and to when computers can be used by just about anyone from the 1980s through today. With the advent of tablet computing and a simple user interface pioneered by Apple, computing capability has been extended to the most elementary of users. It has been speculated that the innovative graphical user interface on the iPad® was a major shift in computing by extending access to the Internet to the widest population possible. Users well into their 70s and 80s today are more active with computing capabilities because the tablet is easy to use.

Naturally, with the expanded use of computers and related IT, we started to see computing become more ingrained in our everyday lives. Where paper products used to suffice, computers offered the ability to go "paperless". Retail operations started taking advantage of the logistics benefits that cyber offered, allowing supply chain management advances that link point-of-sale data, warehouse inventory and real-time sales together that improves supply chain efficiency resulting in time savings, more cost-effective inventory management and improved product forecasting. Healthcare organizations centralize patient medical information, as well as payment and identity data, to gain the same efficiencies enjoyed by the retail profession. As a result, you can set up a doctor's appointment on-line and see the results of the tests and examinations in as little as a day later.

The Department of Defense has been one of the leading government organizations involved with computing technologies. The former Advanced Research Projects Agency or ARPA developed the concept for a shared packet-switched based network of computing systems in 1967. This was the foundation for today's Internet. It was the first network to implement the Transmission Control Protocol/Internet Protocol suite or as it is simply referred to today as TCP/IP. Since much of our information started moving onto computer systems and networks, it was only a matter of time when we would need to protect them. As shared in Chapter 1, there were some major events that started us all focusing on protecting our data and computers.

Computer security, as a discipline, became a seriously studied topic in the early 1970s. Papers by such authors as James P. Anderson, David E. Bell and Leonard J. LaPadula, Richard Bisbey II, James Carlstedt, Dennis Hollingworth, and Peter G. Neumann provided foundational research in aspects of software assurance, trusted computing standards, trusting read/write processes to differing classification levels, and operating system security that drove doctrine, policy, standards, and directives throughout the government. One can go to the National Institute of Science and Technology website and browse many of these historic documents – including the DoD Trusted Computer System Evaluation Criteria or "Orange Book". It was called the "Orange Book" because of the deep orange cover paper used in the print version. The other standards in the series were intentionally given colorful covers (i.e., the "Green Book" on password management, the "Light Yellow Book" on applying computer security requirements, the "Yellow Book" on the technical rationale behind the requirements, and the "Red Book" on the trusted network interpretation), which became commonly referred to as the "Rainbow Series". While the standards are not current, they form the foundation of thought and policy that applies even today.[3]

Recent Developments in Cybersecurity

Today's standards and policies have evolved and changed to keep up with technology and growth of information systems and networks throughout government and private industry. Cyber, and its related impacts to daily life, has become the preeminent concern today. As noted in Chapter 1, there has been a concerted effort to define exactly what we mean when we say, "cyber". While you can find some specific definitions in this chapter and in **Appendix A**, in this section we will introduce the terms and definitions evolving and in current use in the industry. **Appendix B** offers a "Rosetta Stone" of terms to assist when applying for certifications; it also provides a basic understanding of how your specific job experiences convert to commercial cybersecurity. To start, we need to understand the term, *cyberspace.* This specific name was first used in a 1984 science fiction novel and defined as:

> "...a consensual hallucination experienced daily by billions of legitimate operators, in every nation, by children being taught mathematical concepts... A graphical representation of data abstracted from the banks of every computer in the human system. Unthinkable complexity. Lines of light ranged in the non-space of the mind, clusters and constellations of data."[4]

Even though Gibson's description seemed esoteric, the concept seemed to resonate with computer hobbyists in the mid-1980s, and eventually crossed over into the mainstream lexicon as computer systems became more and more important to our daily lives. From at least 1997 onward, the definition and related lexicons evolved and changed as various stakeholders attempted to categorize cyber, often times producing simultaneous and contradictory documents.

President George W. Bush signed the *National Strategy to Secure Cyberspace* (Figure 3.1) in 2003[5] in which cyberspace was described as "...composed of hundreds of thousands of interconnected computers, servers, routers, switches, and fiber optic cables that allow our critical infrastructures to work." The formal strategy essentially focused on the aspects of cyberspace that comprised what was called the backbone of the nation's critical information infrastructure that was described as:

Figure 3.1 | National Strategy to Secure Cyberspace

> "...public and private institutions in the sectors of agriculture, food, water, public health, emergency services, government, defense industrial base, information and telecommunications, energy, transportation, banking and finance, chemicals and hazardous materials, and postal and shipping. Cyberspace is their nervous system—the control system of our country."

It was apparent that government policy focused on the concept that cyberspace comprised the information infrastructure and related components that provided the capability to conduct business, provide supplies and resources, execute financial transactions, and a cognitive understanding of each of those in a near-real time. Because the nation and the nation's military relied so heavily on cyberspace capabilities, the vulnerabilities to which these resources were subject became a national defense priority. What could be vulnerable could be attacked and must be defended.

Conversely, knowing adversaries had the same cyberspace capabilities - and vulnerabilities - meant national military objectives could also be achieved through cyberspace. The *National Military Strategy for Cyberspace Operations*[6] (Figure 3.2) quoted from the 2004 edition of *Joint Publication 1-02, The Department of Defense Dictionary of Military and Associated Terms*[7] in which cyberspace is defined as the "notional environment in which digitized information is communicated over computer networks". However, it was determined that the quoted definition was too limiting and provided a new definition in which cyberspace was defined as a "*...domain* [emphasis added] characterized by the use of electronics and the electromagnetic spectrum to store, modify, and exchange data via networked systems and associated physical infrastructures."

Figure 3.2 | National Military Strategy for Cyberspace Operations

The use of the term, *domain*, indicated the inclusion of cyber into the operational environment war-fighting domains. To clarify, *Joint Publication 5-0, Joint Operations Planning*[8] describes the operational environment as:

> "...the composite of the conditions, circumstances, and influences that affect the employment of capabilities and bear on the decisions of the commander. It encompasses physical areas and factors of the air, land, maritime, and space domains and the information environment (which includes cyberspace) ..."

In the effort to include cyberspace into the warfighting domain, the military services began to evaluate the specific mission responsibilities that could be executed, if tasked. However, as mentioned in Chapter 1, the concern that the definition was too militarized so the formal definition was again changed in 2011 to "...an *operational* [emphasis added] domain to organize, train, and equip so that DoD can take full advantage of cyberspace's potential."[9] In 2012, the DoD defined its cyberspace workforce as:

> "...personnel who perform cyberspace functions in direct support of the cyberspace domain to architect, engineer, securely provision, operate, maintain, protect, defend, analyze, manage information or information systems; investigate cyberspace activities; conduct specialized cyberspace operations; conduct law enforcement or counter intelligence operations, develop cyberspace policy, conduct portfolio management, educate, train, or provide legal counsel."

One only need read through all the verbal roles to see that the workforce was defined to be broad and all encompassing. The specifics in the defined workforce, however, aligns with the **National Initiative for Cybersecurity Education (NICE)** framework which was initiated in 2010 (Figure 3.3).[10] NICE, which is led by the National Institute of Standards and Technology (NIST) in the U.S. Department of Commerce, is a partnership between government, academia, and the private sector working to energize and promote a robust network and an ecosystem of cybersecurity education, training, and workforce development.

Figure 3.3 | NICE

With all this change in terms, the question arises about *cybersecurity.* As noted above, the concern about securing computers began in earnest in 1979. The term at the time was direct – *computer security* or COMPUSEC. The thought was the approach to secure all aspects of the computing environment seemed pretty straightforward.

Roughly six to eight years later, the term changed to *information security* or INFOSEC, because the approach shifted to focus on the *information* stored and processed on computer systems, or as they were starting to be called, *IT systems.* This was the term used mostly within the Federal government and later adopter by industry, when the responsibility of organizations to label the classification of information as well as to define the protection requirements was starting to be confused with the protection, detection, reaction, and response actions taken to defend information on computers.

As a result of the functional role debate, the term was changed around 1990 to *information assurance* or IA; the thought being that the intent and effort is to assure that information was kept confidential when required, kept available for authorized use, and the integrity was maintained to ensure accuracy and accountability. IA was also the term most used to define the workforce, functions, and policies surrounding the security efforts focused on information on what was later called "information systems". The term, though widely understood, seemed to need to adapt to the "new" world of *cyber.*

Direction from the Office of the President in 2008 changed information assurance to *cybersecurity* and defined it specifically as "...prevention of damage to, protection of, and restoration of computers, electronic communications systems, electronic communication services, wire communications, and electronic communication, including information contained therein, to ensure its availability, integrity, authentication, confidentiality, and non-repudiation".[11] There remains an interesting discussion of whether it is one word, e.g., *cybersecurity,* or two words, e.g., *cyber security.* References in Federal policy and congressional language tend to largely use the one-word pattern, so that is the pattern used in this book.

It seems clear, if nothing else, that the dynamic nature of the profession continues to have stakeholders persistently re-think the terms and roles about every 10 years. As we look to the future, we can be assured that we will see more terms evolve. The best advice is to keep current on readings and "hang on".

What You Need to Know

As mentioned earlier in this book, military members who have an interest in cybersecurity likely come with a significant amount of knowledge, skills and abilities in computer/information system, communications technology, and software. Many can already demonstrate familiarity with the fundamental capabilities of computers, software, information systems, and communications systems.

Notwithstanding, not everyone entering into the cybersecurity career field will be an IT guru. There are numerous positions within cybersecurity career field that require significant knowledge of IT and cybersecurity, but do not require you to be highly technical. Functions such as management, planning, policy analysis, purchasing, and acquisition within the cybersecurity community must be performed, representing over 30% of cybersecurity positions.

However, if you desire to stay at the cutting edge of the cybersecurity career field and continue to grow and develop, you must continually educate yourself and seek certification. Because of the persistent nature of IT in both personal and professional lives, one already easily understands terminology and function of common computer, software, information and communication technology devices, components, and concepts. To transition to the cybersecurity field, there is an expectation that one develops a deeper understanding and ability to efficiently use these capabilities.

It all starts with the technology. This is probably not unexpected, but one truly needs to understand the depth and breadth of experience and knowledge needed to function well in the career field. Later sections will show where some of these skills can be acquired, but to set the stage, the specific areas are provided to manage expectations. Going beyond the familiarity of the every-day user, cybersecurity professionals will need to have a comprehensive understanding of hardware, software, and communication capabilities to perform tasks and communicate effectively. The expectation is that the cybersecurity professional, while not necessarily a singular master, must be that "jack-of-all trades" in the many attributes of hardware, software, and networking/ communications.

To help frame some specific knowledge, skills, and abilities expected of someone moving into the cybersecurity profession, the following section describes cybersecurity workforce skills within three basic IT groups of hardware, software, and networks to frame the level of education, training, and experience one should obtain to be successful.

1. Hardware

Cybersecurity professionals need to demonstrate competence with such specific hardware technology as the central processing unit (CPU), including implementing protection attributes in the Trusted Processing Modules (TPM). This also includes an understanding the functions of both random-access memory (RAM) and read-only memory (ROM), as well as an understanding of the attributes and impacts of various storage media, (e.g., internal hard disk, external hard disk, network drive, solid-state hard drives, CD, DVD, USB, flash drive, and memory cards). Related to the CPU and storage, there has to be an understanding of how input/output ports, (e.g., USB, serial, parallel, network port, FireWire) function and what vulnerabilities may be inherent, along with input devices, (e.g., mouse; keyboard; trackball; scanner; touchpad; stylus; joystick; web camera; digital camera; microphone; voice recognition; remote control; gesture/motion; haptics; and head, mouth, and eye operated controllers) and output devices, (e.g., screens/monitors, printers, speakers, headphones, wearable computing).

With the convergence of Operational Technologies (OT) – devices, sensors and software necessary to control and monitor plant and equipment – with IT in general, the cybersecurity professional is going to have to rise to the challenge to understand and differentiate between IT and OT architectures and the operation of these architectures. The particular blending of industrial control systems onto the IT backbone has unique security issues of which the cybersecurity professional needs to be aware.

2. Software

The cybersecurity professional will have the experience and knowledge of software technology such as **operating systems, database management systems,** and **cryptography,** and are further described below.

Operating systems are varied and tend to fall into three general categories: Windows-based (bother server and host-based versions), Unix-based (with all of the flavors Red Hat, SUSE, Debian, Ubuntu, GNU, Open BSD, and others), and Apple-based (or Mac-OS) products. With the explosion in mobile technologies, all three of these general operating systems have mobile flavors. For example, the Android OS is a general variant of the Unix-based operating system, and Apple has Apple iOS for their mobile devices. With Windows 10, Microsoft is starting the blend the host-based and mobile-based operating system construct for their product line, even adding Linux command options (e.g., Brian Fox's "bourne-again shell" or *bash*). Virtualization is also a major capability affecting the operating system environments. As more and more systems virtualize, the cybersecurity professional will need to understand risks and protections affecting the hypervisor, and threats of data leakage in virtual systems.

Database management systems (DBMS) also come in a variety of types, depending upon their database management structure. The most prevalent are Relational DBMS with products such as Oracle, Informix, Sybase, and both Microsoft SQL Server and Access. Cybersecurity professionals will need to understand the capabilities and functionality associated with various technologies for organizing and managing information (e.g., databases, bookmarking engines) and show they understand database management systems, query languages, table relationships, and views. As a result, cybersecurity professionals should understand data classification standards and methodologies based on sensitivity and other risk factors when data is aggregated in databases. This would also include understand what sensitive information an organization may have, where it resides, and who needs access to it. The expectation would be that the cybersecurity professional would have knowledge of advanced data remediation security features in databases, and how to implement and manage them.

Because **cryptography** is such a powerful and important element in cybersecurity, one who is coming into the field should be able to explain the core concepts of cryptography and cryptographic key management concepts. It is not being suggested that one needs to become a math "wiz"; however, there must also be a solid understanding of the concept and implementation of public key infrastructure (PKI) and other encryption methodologies. Specifically, there must be a comprehensive understand of key authentication, authorization, and access control principles and methods. The cybersecurity professional should be able to explain the need for access authentication controls, including the need to disable expired user accounts and regularly change passwords. They should also understand the protections needed for Personally Identifiable Information (PII).

Cybersecurity professionals will need to understand and demonstrate how the security aspects of the operating systems, database management systems, and cryptography can be managed, controlled, implemented, and defended. This implies an inherent understanding of the security controls in each. It also provides an expectation of the interrelationship of each can provide layers of additional protection and reduce risk. Software assurance reviews have recently become a requirement from Congress,[12] so being able to apply cybersecurity principles and methods software development has become a required skill.

3. Networks

Networks are the backbone of the environment – no pun intended. For data to be safely communicated across cyberspace, networking concepts and protocols, and network security methodologies must be clearly understood. As a result, it is expected that a cybersecurity professional would be comfortable explaining network design processes, to include the understanding of security objectives, operational objectives, and tradeoffs. They should be able to explain local area network (LAN) and wide area network (WAN) principles and concepts, including bandwidth management. While it might not appear to be directly security related, a cybersecurity professional should have a keen understanding of service management concepts for networks and related standards (e.g., IT Infrastructure Library, v3 [ITIL]).

A cybersecurity professional should be able to identify the range of existing networks types within the organization, explain how traffic flows across the network, and explain server administration and systems engineering theories, concepts, and methods. They should understand the information flow down to the packet level. They should also have the skills and ability to identify and implement host and network access control mechanisms (e.g., access control list), and have the knowledge of basic system administration, network, and operating system hardening techniques.

As more technologies begin to collapse onto the network, it becomes more important to understand Voice over Internet Protocols (VoIPs) and the impact of VoIP upon the organizations infrastructure. Since web technologies are the connection points to an organizations information with the outside world, then a cybersecurity professional needs to understand web services, including service oriented architecture, Representational State Transfer (REST), Simple Object Access Protocol (SOAP), and web service description language. With cloud technologies becoming more common, the cybersecurity professional will be expected to know more about cloud-based knowledge management technologies and concepts related to security, governance, procurement, and administration.

The core attribute of a cybersecurity professional's job is security and risk management. The knowledge of the hardware, software, and networking technical constructs is foundational, but the cybersecurity professional is expected to take that knowledge and combine it with a comprehensive understand of emerging security issues, risks, and vulnerabilities to provide a secure and functional cyber environment. This is where the *art* and *science* of cybersecurity begins to blend.

There are certain concepts which can be outlined, checklists and standard from which to measure; in other words, the *science* of the technology. However, the judicious implementation of a balanced, mission-focused, risk management program will often be found in the *art* of the profession. A basic understanding of the principles and organizational requirements that are relevant to confidentiality, integrity, availability, authentication, and non-repudiation attributes for the organizations networks are key; and from that understanding there is an expectation that the cybersecurity professional will be able to apply the confidentiality, availability, and integrity principles consistently.

Part of the role of a cybersecurity professional is to develop the information exchanges and sources to be able to identify emerging computer-based technology that has potential for exploitation by adversaries. This implies a constant study/reading regimen to keep up on the new and emerging cybersecurity technologies and trends, and to develop proposed solutions. It also includes understanding the products and nomenclature of major IT security vendors and how differences affect exploitation, vulnerabilities, and mitigations. This persistent pursuit of knowledge will contribute in the ability to determine how a security system should work – including its resilience and dependability capabilities – and how changes in conditions, operations, or the environment will affect these outcomes.

A skill often overlooked is the ability to explain key concepts in cybersecurity management issues, e.g., release management, patch management, the Assessment and Authorization (A&A) process, to management. Cybersecurity professionals are often called upon to explain backup and storage requirements and procedures, limited access requirements, or the concept of digital rights management to organizational leadership. The issue becomes stressful when the terminology used is very technical – commonly called "geek-speak" – and leadership doesn't understand what is being expressed. A cybersecurity professional should be well versed in the mission (or business) of the organization, and be able to eloquently link the cybersecurity concepts to the mission or business result.

Cybersecurity Core Functions

With skills in hardware, software, networks, and so forth, one would ask…what am I expected to actually be able to DO?!? The Department of Commerce's National Institute of Standards and Technology (NIST) led the National Initiative for Cybersecurity Education (NICE) and created a publication called the NICE Cybersecurity Workforce Framework (NCWF). This framework presents five essential core functions that provide a set of activities needed to achieve specific cybersecurity outcomes. These outcomes cross all roles within cybersecurity, which will be addressed in the next section. Figure 3.4 below lists the five core functions and provides some references examples of guidance to achieve those outcomes.

Cybersecurity Core Functions

Identify	This is defined as the function needed develop the organizational understanding to manage cybersecurity risk to systems, assets, data, and capabilities. This includes those functions that help one understand the business context, the resources that support critical functions, and the related cybersecurity risks which enable an organization to focus and prioritize its efforts, consistent with its risk management strategy and business needs.
Protect	This is defined as the function needed to develop and implement the appropriate safeguards to ensure delivery of critical infrastructure services, and the ability to limit or contain the impact of a potential cybersecurity event.
Detect	This is defined as the function needed for one to develop and implement the appropriate activities to identify the occurrence of a cybersecurity event through the timely discovery of cybersecurity events.
Respond	This is defined as the function one needs to develop and implement the **appropriate** activities to **take action** regarding a detected cybersecurity event, thus supporting the ability to contain the impact of a potential cybersecurity event.
Recover	This is defined as the functions needed to develop and implement the **appropriate** activities to **maintain** plans for resilience and to restore any capabilities or services that were impaired due to a cybersecurity event. This is key to supporting timely recovery to normal operations, thus reducing the impact from a cybersecurity event.

Figure 3.4 | Cybersecurity Core Functions

The cybersecurity core functions[13] start by noting the organization needs to ***identify*** the cybersecurity functions and capabilities in order to determine potential risk to their systems and assets. With that information, the organization will be able to implement the appropriate measures to ***protect*** the system, have the ability to ***detect*** when anomalies happen, to ***respond*** appropriately, and be resilient enough to ***recover*** from whatever impairment caused by the anomaly. When the functions are considered together, they provide a broad, strategic view of the organization's lifecycle management of cybersecurity risk. This is done through a formal risk management process.

Cybersecurity Workforce Framework

The *Cybersecurity Workforce* is defined as those personnel who secure, defend and preserve data, networks, net-centric capabilities, and other designated systems by ensuring appropriate security controls and measures are in place, and taking internal defense actions. This includes access to system controls, monitoring, administration and integration of cybersecurity into all aspects of engineering and acquisition of cyberspace capabilities. These roles are the focus of this section.

Within the DoD cyberspace workforce construct, there are three major ***lines of operation*** for the cybersecurity professional. These are **Defensive Cyberspace Operations** (DCO), **DoD Information Network (DODIN) operations**, and **cyberspace capabilities support.** There is a distinctive flavor of detect, react, and respond functions in each line of operation to assure the protection and defense of the cyberspace environment; however, one can see how the overarching cyberspace workforce responsibilities are intertwined in each.

DCO describes both passive and active cyberspace operations intended to preserve the ability to use friendly cyberspace capabilities and protect data, networks, net-centric capabilities, and other designated systems. This role would be found at security operations centers, data centers, and a variety of IT centers. This easily translates into industry, as they have similar functions.

DODIN Operations defines more of the business and sustainment operations. This function has roles and responsibilities to design, build, configure, secure, operate, maintain, and sustain DoD networks in order to create and preserve information assurance on DoD information networks. Again, industry has similar functions and roles for their own industrial or corporate infrastructure.

The **cyberspace capabilities support** functions are those positions where actions are taken to oversee and manage cybersecurity capabilities. This includes; cyberspace policy, prioritizing portfolio investments, architecture, engineering, acquisition, implementation, and disposal of IT and services. It would also include information resources management, the storage, transmission, and display of data and information, and training of cybersecurity workforce personnel. As the other two functions, there are similar roles in both corporate and commercial industry environments.

When one compares each of the specific lines of operation with the cyberspace workforce definitions, it is clear to see that elements of the cyberspace workforce responsibilities are contained in their descriptions. This is not necessarily contradictory. Research has shown that the concern by the war-fighters and other business system owners – the ultimate customers of cyberspace capabilities – are more concerned with the continued safe and secure operations of their network resources.[14]

The NICE Cybersecurity Workforce Framework (Figure 3.5) works "... to provide a common understanding of and lexicon for cybersecurity work..." in order to ensure the ability "...to educate, recruit, train, develop, and retain a highly-qualified workforce."[15] There are seven specific categories that have workforce titles and associated job descriptions. Because you are transitioning from the military services, in this

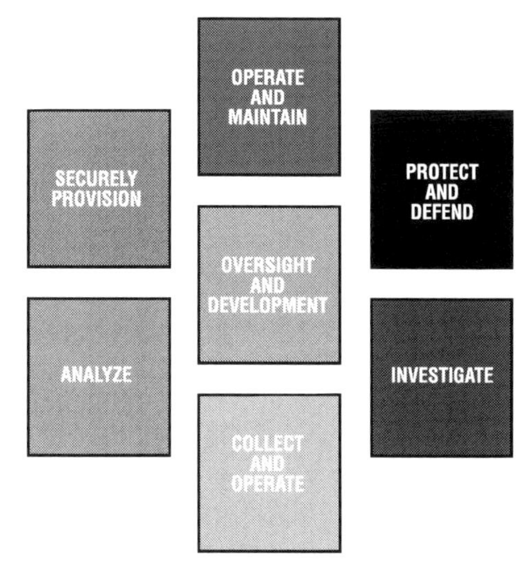

Figure 3.5 | Cybersecurity Workforce Framework

book we will use the NICE Framework, but they are still very close to the NICE definitions and can be easily related if one is looking to work in the civil agencies or the supporting industries.

To ensure that the functions of identify, protect, detect, respond, and recover are executed across an organization, the Cybersecurity Workforce Framework categories contain roles and responsibilities and related tasks that allow individuals to find their comfortable niche, and permit management to hire to the overall need of the organization. These categories contain elements of skills and abilities for the workforce to ensure the cybersecurity core functions are addressed.

This section of chapter 3 is where the rubber meets the road. Read through these categories to learn and understand what encompasses these jobs. A series of actual job roles/titles are listed further providing alignment when looking at positions. Note: These lists do not present all job titles or roles. Our intent here is to share examples for clarity, and to help you navigate towards a *particular* job that uses your experience and piques your specific interests. One item of note—you will still see the term "Information Assurance" or IA as a descriptor for a number of the role titles that follow. Even though the term has officially changed to "cybersecurity", there still remains residual use of the older term. This should not be considered a different skill set or responsibility.

As you look at the job title examples, you will see some fall into more than one specialty area, especially some of the more senior positions like the Chief Information Security Officer (CISO). This is because their responsibilities are often more strategic and have broader influences. You will also see some examples with no specific job title list because either the specialty is the title or because the specialty can only be filled by a certain skill set (e.g., lawyers, law enforcement officer). As it turns out, this list also includes (in italics) those same job titles that are part of the cyber IT workforce—which tend to cross over into both career fields (for more detail in that career, see ***The Transitioning Military IT Professional*** book).

1. Securely Provision

In the **Securely Provision** specialties, individuals with risk management responsibilities oversee, evaluate, and support the documentation, validation, and accreditation processes necessary to assure that new systems meet the organization's cybersecurity requirements. In these roles, one ensures the appropriate treatment of risk, compliance, and assurance from internal and external perspectives.

Secure Acquisition roles manage and support the acquisition life cycle, including planning, determining specifications, selecting, and procuring information and communications technology (ICT) and cybersecurity products used in the organization's design, development, and maintenance of its infrastructure to minimize potential risks and vulnerabilities. Some job titles that might have **Secure Acquisition** roles would be:

Chief Information Security Officer (CISO)	Contracting Officer Technical Representative (COTR)
Contracting Officer (CO)	IT Director

Secure Software Engineers develop, modify, enhance, and sustains new or existing computer applications, software, or utility programs following software assurance best practices throughout the software lifecycle. Some job titles associated with the **Secure Software Engineer** role would be:

Analyst Programmer	Computer Programmer
Configuration Manager	Database Developer/ Engineer/ Architect
Cybersecurity Engineer	Cybersecurity Software Developer
Cybersecurity Software Engineer	Research & Development Engineer
Secure Software Engineer	Security Engineer
Software Developer	Software Engineer/Architect
Systems Analyst	Web Application Developer

Systems Security Architects design and develop system concepts and works on the capabilities phases of the systems development lifecycle. They translate technology and environmental conditions (e.g., laws, regulations, best practices) into system and security designs and processes. Some job titles that would have **System Security Architect** responsibilities would include:

Information Assurance (IA) Architect	Security Architect
Information Security Architect	Security Engineer
Information Systems Security Engineer	Security Solutions Architect
Network Security AnalystSystems	Systems Engineer
Research & Development Engineer	Systems Security Analyst

Technology Research and Development personnel conduct technology and/or feasibility assessments. Individuals in this role would provide, build, and support a prototype capability and/or evaluates its security and utility. In this role, the individual would be key in the effort to facilitate innovation. Job titles represented in the **Technology Research and Development** area are:

Capabilities and Development Specialist	Chief Engineer
Research & Development Engineer	Research & Development Research Engineer

Systems Requirements Planner responsibilities consist primarily of consulting with stakeholders to guide, gather, and evaluate functional and security requirements. It also requires the ability to translate these requirements into guidance to stakeholders about the applicability of information systems to meet their needs. Some of the tasks one would expect a Systems Requirements Planner to do would be to integrate and align information security and/or IA policies to ensure system analysis meets security requirements; manage IT projects to ensure that developed solutions meet customer requirements; oversee and make recommendations regarding configuration management; and perform needs analysis to determine opportunities for new and improved business process solutions. Job titles associated with **Systems Requirements Planner** responsibilities would include:

Business Analyst	Business Process Analyst
Computer Systems Analyst	Human Factors Engineer
Requirements Analyst	Solutions Architect
Systems Consultant	Systems Engineer

Test and Evaluation roles are focused on developing and conducting processes and procedures (e.g., testing) to evaluate compliance with security requirements. This requires a very disciplined and organized mind-set. Some of the more specific tasks would include analyzing the results of end-to-end testing (e.g., software, hardware, transport, seams, interfaces); determining the level of assurance of developed capabilities based on test results; developing test plans to address specifications and requirements, and providing recommendations based on those test results. Job titles most recognized **Test and Evaluation** would include:

Application Security Tester	Information Systems Security Engineer
Quality Assurance (QA) Tester	Research & Development Engineer
Research & Development Research Engineer	Security Systems Engineer
Software Quality Assurance (QA) Engineer	Software Quality Engineer
Systems Engineer	Testing and Evaluation Specialist

Systems Developers have some of the *broadest* and most far-reaching responsibilities in the Securely Provision function. Individuals in this field are responsible for the development of technical security solutions to meet the defined mission/business and security requirements. Some of the specific tasks would include analyzing design constraints, trade-offs, and detailed system and security designs to identify necessary lifecycle support: assessing the effectiveness of information protection measures utilized by system(s) as well as the threats to and vulnerabilities of computer system(s) to develop a security risk profile; conducting Privacy Impact Analysis (PIA) of the applications security design for the appropriate security controls, which protect the confidentiality and integrity of Personal Identifiable Information (PII); designing, developing, integrating, and updating system security measures (including policies and requirements) that provide confidentiality, integrity, availability, authentication, and non-repudiation; and developing detailed security design documentation. The job title of **System Developer** is pretty much the primary term used.

2. Operate & Maintain

In the **Operate & Maintain** roles, individuals provide the support, administration, and maintenance necessary to ensure effective and efficient IT system performance and security. They configure, secure, operate and maintain networks to create and preserve the information assurance conditions and standards. Most of the roles, e.g., Data Administration, Customer Service & Tech Support, Network Services, and System Administrators can be found in more detail in the ***The Transitioning Military IT Professional*** book. The role of System Security Analysis, though listed under the **Operate & Maintain** area, focuses primarily on cybersecurity responsibilities.

Systems Security Analysis is the role where one would conduct and document the systems integration, testing, operations, maintenance, and security of an information environment. This responsibility includes coordinating threat and mitigation strategies across the enterprise. The job titles where one would be doing **Systems Security Analysis** would include:

Information Assurance (IA)/Cybersecurity Operational Engineer	Information Systems Security Officer
Information Security Analyst/Administrator	Information Security Manager
Information Security Specialist	Information Systems Security Engineer
Information Systems Security Manager	Platform Specialist
Security Administrator	Security Analyst
Security Control Assessor	Security Engineer

3. Oversight and Development

Individuals with these roles are responsible for providing leadership, management, direction, or development and advocacy so the organization may effectively conduct cybersecurity work. The following define Oversight and Development:

Legal Advocacy & Advice personnel provide legal advice and recommendations to leadership and staff on relevant topics within the pertinent subject domain. These **attorneys and legal aides** advocate for legal and policy changes, and makes a case on behalf of the client via written and oral work products, including legal briefs and proceedings. They prepare legal documents (e.g., depositions, briefs, affidavits, declarations, appeals, pleadings, and discovery), as well as providing legal interpretations regarding laws, regulations, policies, standards, or procedures. These individuals would be lawyers and other in the legal profession.

Training, Education & Awareness roles include the responsibility to develop, plan, coordinate, deliver, and/or evaluate instructional cybersecurity content using various formats, techniques, and venues. These individuals would be filling job titles that would include:

Cyber Trainer	Information Security Trainer
Cybersecurity Instructor	System Security Trainer
Systems Instructor	Security Training Coordinator

Strategic Planning and Policy Development roles would have individuals responsible for applying technical and organizational knowledge to define an entity's strategic direction, determining resource allocations, establishing priorities, and identifying programs or infrastructure required to achieve desired goals. These individuals develop policy or are advocates for policy change that supports new initiatives or required changes and enhancements. These responsibilities would *also* include the **Executive Cyberspace Leadership.** These individuals establish organizational priorities and strategic direction, determine resource allocation, and identify programs or infrastructures that are required to achieve goals within a domain of interest. These leaders oversee and supervise the execution of cyberspace policies, missions, and functions oftentimes for a broad organization. Samples of job titles for all in this specialty would include:

Information Security Policy Analyst	Information Security Policy Manager
Policy Writer and Strategist	Cybersecurity Planner
Chief Information Officer (CIO)	Chief Information Security Officer (CISO)
Command Information Officer	Senior Information Security Official (SISO)

Cybersecurity Management responsibilities are those roles which oversee the cybersecurity program of an information system or network; including managing information security implications within the organization, specific program, or other area of responsibility, to include strategic, personnel, infrastructure, requirements, policy enforcement, emergency planning, security awareness, and other resources. Job titles that would include these roles would include:

Chief Information Security Officer (CISO)	Common Control Provider
Cybersecurity Officer	Enterprise Security Officer
Facility Security Officer	Information Systems Security Manager (ISSM)
IT Director	Principal Security Architect
Risk Executive	Security Domain Specialist
Senior Agency Information Security (SAIS) Officer	Senior Information Security Official (SISO)

Risk Management roles include those responsibilities to oversee, evaluate, and support the documentation, validation, and accreditation processes necessary to ensure new and existing IT systems meet the organization's cybersecurity as well as other security discipline requirements. These individuals would be responsible for ensuring the appropriate treatment of risk, compliance, and monitoring assurance from internal and external perspectives. The job titles one would expect to see having these roles and responsibilities would include:

Accreditor	Authorizing Official
Analyst/Manager	Auditor
Authorizing Official Designated Representative	Certification Agent
Certifying Official	Compliance Manager
Designated Accrediting Authority	Information Assurance (IA) Auditor
Information Assurance (IA) Compliance	Senior Certification Authority
Information System Security Manager (ISSM)	Information System Security Officer (ISSO)
Information Assurance (IA) Officer Portfolio Manager	Quality Assurance (QA) Specialist
Risk/Vulnerability Analyst	Security Control Assessor
Systems Analyst	Validator

Knowledge Management roles include overseeing and administering integrated methods, enabling the organization to identify, capture, catalog, classify, retrieve, and share intellectual capital and information content. These methods may include processes and tools (e.g., databases, documents, policies, procedures) and human expertise pertaining to the organization. Some of the more specific tasks would include administering the indexing/cataloguing, storage, and access of organizational documents; developing an understanding of the needs and requirements of information end-users; monitoring and reporting the usage of knowledge management assets and resources; and promoting knowledge sharing through an organization's operational processes and systems by strengthening links between knowledge sharing and IT systems. Job titles that have this role or responsibility would include:

Business Analyst	Business Intelligence Manager
Content Administrator	Document Steward
Freedom of Information Act Official	Information Manager
Information Owner	Information Resources Manager
Knowledge Manager	Information Manager

4. Protect & Defend

Individuals in the Protect & Defend specialty areas would be responsible for identifying, analyzing, and mitigating threats to internal IT systems or networks.

Computer/Enterprise Network Defense (C/END) Analysis is the role where one would test, implement, deploy, maintain, review, and administer the infrastructure hardware, software, and documentation required to effectively manage network defense resources. These personnel monitor the network to actively remediate unauthorized activities. Some of the specific job titles that would be expected to fulfil this role would include:

Computer Network Defense (CND) Analyst (Cryptologic)	Cybersecurity Intelligence Analyst
Enterprise Network Defense (END) Analyst	Focused Operations Analyst
Incident Analyst	Network Defense Technician
Network Security Engineer	Security Analyst, Security Operator
Sensor Analyst	END Infrastructure Support
Incident Response	Vulnerability Assessment & Management Analyst

Computer/Enterprise Network Defense (C/END) Infrastructure Support responsibilities include employees who test, implement, deploy, maintain, review, and administer the infrastructure hardware, software, and documentation required to effectively manage network defense resources. This role also monitors the network to actively remediate unauthorized activities.

Computer Network Defense (CND) Specialist	Cybersecurity Intelligence Analyst
Enterprise Network Defense (END) Specialist	Systems Operations Defense Specialist
Incident Responder	Incident Handler
Incident Response Coordinator	Security Analyst, Security Operator
Vulnerability Assessment & Management Analyst	END Infrastructure Support
Network Defense Technician	Network Security Engineer

Incident Response responsibilities include roles where one responds to disruptions within the pertinent domain to mitigate immediate and potential threats. These personnel use mitigation, preparedness, and response and recovery approaches to maximize survival of life, preservation of property, and information security. They would do some preliminary investigation and analysis on relevant response activities and evaluate the effectiveness of and improvements to existing practices. Job titles for this area would include:

Computer Crime Investigator	Incident Handler
Incident Responder	Incident Response Analyst
Incident Response Coordinator	Intrusion Analyst

Vulnerability Assessment and Management roles include those responsibilities for conducting threat and vulnerability assessments and determining any deviations from acceptable configurations or policies. These personnel would be responsible for assessing the level of risk and developing and/or recommending appropriate mitigations and countermeasures for operational and non-operational situations. Job titles that would be expected to fulfill these roles would include:

Blue Team Technician	Certified TEMPEST Professional or Certified TEMPEST Technical Authority (CTTA)
Close Access Technician	Computer or Enterprise Network Defense (CND/END) Auditor
Compliance Manager	Ethical Hacker
Governance Manager	Information Security Engineer
Internal Enterprise Auditor	Network Security Engineer
Penetration Tester	Red Team Technician
Reverse Engineer	Risk/Vulnerability Analyst
Technical Surveillance Countermeasures Technician	Vulnerability Manager

5. Investigate

Individuals working in the Investigation specialty areas would be ***law enforcement or counter-intelligence*** agents who would have the responsibility for investigating cyber events or crimes related to IT systems, networks, and digital evidence.

Cyber Investigation responsibilities would include those skills in applying the tactics, techniques, and procedures with a full range of tools and processes related to administrative, criminal, and counter intelligence gathering (e.g., in-depth case analyses, continuous monitoring, malware analysis, clear documentation). This is primarily the work of **Special Agents** (either Law Enforcement or Counter Intelligence) or other **credentialed Computer Crime Investigators.** Bottom-line, for this job you will need a badge.

Digital Forensics include those responsibilities to collect, process, preserve, analyze, and present digital-related evidence to support network vulnerability mitigation and/or civil, workplace, counterintelligence, or law enforcement (e.g., criminal, fraud) investigations. While the job titles of those working digital forensics would include Special Agents and Computer Crime Investigators, one would also expect to see others with this responsibility, such as:

Computer Forensic Analyst	Computer/Enterprise Network Defense (E/CND) Forensic Analyst
Digital Forensic Examiner	Digital Media Collector
Forensic Analyst	Forensic Analyst (Cryptologic)
Forensic Technician	Network Forensic Examiner

6. Analyze

For the purposes of the Cybersecurity Workforce Framework, these Specialty Areas are primarily associated with ***intelligence*** responsibilities, and they include highly specialized review and evaluation skills for incoming cybersecurity information to determine its usefulness for intelligence. *Without specifying any specific job title*, these roles would include:

Threat Analysis roles would be those that require the ability and skill to identify and assess the capabilities and activities of cyber criminals or foreign intelligence entities. These individuals would then produce findings to help initialize or support law enforcement and counterintelligence investigations or activities.

Exploitation Analysis roles would include the skills to analyze collected information to identify vulnerabilities and potential for exploitation.

All-Source Analysis roles would analyze threat information from multiple sources, disciplines, and agencies across the Intelligence Community; and then synthesizes and places intelligence information in context to draw insights about the possible implications.

Target job roles would include the ability to apply current knowledge of one or more regions, countries, non-state entities, and/or technologies.

7. Operate & Collect

Again, for the purposes of the Cybersecurity Workforce Framework, these Specialty Areas are primarily associated with skills and capabilities for specialized denial and deception operations and the collection of cybersecurity information that may be used to develop intelligence. *Without specifying any specific job title*, these roles would include:

Collection Operations roles would execute collection using appropriate strategies within the priorities established through the collection management process.

Cyber Operational Planning would be roles to performs in-depth joint targeting and cyber planning process. These individuals would gather information and develop detailed operational plans and orders supporting requirements. They would also conduct strategic and operational-level planning across the full range of operations for integrated information and cyberspace operations.

Cyber Operations roles include the responsibility to perform activities to gather evidence on criminal or foreign intelligence entities to mitigate possible or real-time threats, protect against espionage or insider threats, foreign sabotage, international terrorist activities, or to support other intelligence activities.

As you can see, there are a wide variety of cybersecurity job roles, functions, and specialties. This just assures there is a lot of work to be done and a wide variety of possible opportunities. To ensure one can be successful, it is important to receive the proper education and training, to go with the experience you have as a veteran.

Education

There are always those who question the validity and need for formal education in the field of cybersecurity. Individuals hold Bill Gates and Mark Zuckerberg up as examples of successful people who didn't finish their college education and were wildly successful; however, we need to remember there are a vast majority of more who didn't finish and are not successful. A degree shows a disciplined approach to education and overall learning. A bachelor's degree demonstrates that one can listen to professors and repeat back the content of the program. It is the baseline measure of an educational experience that industry expects. A master's degree is the first level of education where the student is to take what was learned and apply independent thought to the material – normally through the thesis process – showing the professor they truly understand the material and are not just parroting it back. A doctorate is where the student actually provides additional knowledge and insight into the field of study through the research and dissertation process.

As a result of the President's concern about cybersecurity, the White House published a Cybersecurity National Action Plan of 2016.[16] In that plan, the President's Budget targeted an investment of $62 million to expand the Scholarship for Service program by establishing a CyberCorps Reserve program, which will offer scholarships for Americans who wish to obtain cybersecurity education and serve their country in the Federal government.[17] Recently, the Federal government published a memo outlining the Federal Cybersecurity

Workforce Strategy.[18] As part of that strategy the White House plans to partner and work with Federal agencies to find ways to streamline the current government hiring practices and leverage existing hiring authorities. There is even a plan to establish a cybersecurity cadre within the Presidential Management Fellows program that would leverage the Presidential Innovation Fellows program as well as others in an attempt to bring cybersecurity practitioners into government service.

Companies and employers in technical fields actively desire some formal education and require a degree; bottom line, get that degree. Depending upon the type of experience obtained while active duty or in the past, some recommended course topics might include those listed in the Figure 3.6 below.

Introduction to Information Systems	PC Hardware and O/S Architecture
Computer and Information Systems	Microcomputer Operating Systems
Introduction to Computer Applications & Concepts	Personal Computer Hardware Troubleshooting
Operating System Fundamentals	Administration of Network Resources
Help Desk Support Skills	VOiP (Voice Over Internet Protocol)
User Support/Help Desk Principles	Introduction to Application Programming Technician

Figure 3.6 | Sample College Course List

There are a number of institutions that offer formal education and related course work in the cybersecurity and other cyberspace operations fields. As before, if you are just starting out in the career and the experience is limited, then attending a local community college or university is an excellent start. The key in your search for the most appropriate college or university to gain an education in cybersecurity is to confirm if the institutions are rated as a *National Center of Academic Excellence* (NCAE) in Information Assurance. One can find schools that are National Centers of Academic Excellence in Information Assurance 2-Year Education rated or CAE/2Y. These are the community colleges in many cities and towns across the country. Four year institutions are rated as National Centers of Academic Excellence in Information Assurance Education or CAE/IAE, National Centers of Academic Excellence in Information Assurance Research or CAE/R, or National Centers of Academic Excellence in Information Assurance (IA)/Cyber Defense (CD). Some of these institutions have been provided in **Appendix D**, but you can find the full list of NCAE rated schools on their website.

College and university courses should have a combination of technology and cybersecurity topics. You should look also look for courses in Computer Forensics, Perimeter Defense procedures, Fundamentals in Firewall and Router Configuration, Risk Assessment and Management, Disaster Recovery and Contingency Planning, and the ever-changing (yet every consistent) topic of Certification and Accreditation processes (now known as Authorization and Approval). Now these courses and topics are just a sample of some that are offered by various educational institutions, which would fit into a cybersecurity career. Other examples would be those listed in the Figure 3.7 below. If you notice, most are directly related to the various functions and roles described earlier.

Computer Forensics/Networks
Computer Science
Cybersecurity Strategy and Policy
Engineering
IT/Risk Management
Cybersecurity/ Information Assurance/Information System Security
Program Management
Information Systems/Technology Management
Supply Chain Management
Network Management
Software Applications & Programming/Development
Systems and Network Auditing
Web Development
Knowledge Management
Hard Sciences/Mathematics
Operations Research
Space Systems

Figure 3.7 | Sample College Course Topics List

While not necessarily saying one should become a lawyer, your schools and studies in cybersecurity should include exposing you to applicable statutory law examples, such as the Electronic Communications Privacy Act (18 U.S.C. §2510-22) ("ECPA"), the Stored Communications Act (18 U.S.C. §2701-110) ("SCA"), and the "Pen/Trap" or Pen Register and Trap & Trace Act (18 U.S.C. §3121-27). You will need to become familiar with legal issues, so a law class here and there is not out of the question. The two example cases (Figure 3.8) show how some case law can impact cybersecurity policy and practices.

O'Connor v. Ortega, 480 U.S. 709 (1987), a significant decision on the Fourth Amendment rights of government employees as it applied to administrative workplace searches by supervisors during investigations for violations of employee policy rather than by law enforcement for criminal offenses. The Supreme Court upheld some of those rights, but only under certain specific conditions .

US v. Long, 64 M.J. 57 (CAAF 2006) and US v. Larson, 64 M.J. 559 (CAAF 2008), two cases where the reasonable expectation of privacy on government systems and in government email access was brought before the court. Both cases were related to criminal activity, and while some privacy was affirmed in US v. Long, it was refuted in US v. Larson.

Figure 3.8 | Cybersecurity Case Law

Training

It really isn't that hard to find training courses for the cybersecurity field; however, the trick is to find those that give one a real "kick start" with a foundation solid enough to help get one through the certification testing process. These tend to fall into two broad ranges: government-provided and commercially-provided. In the case of some of the government training opportunities, the cost may be minimal or completely free – the only condition is that one must currently be in the government either as a uniformed member or a government civilian. The civilian options are more varied and there is a cost associated. Some of the vendors, however, have a guarantee that the students will pass the certification connected to the course taught by offering remedial courses and a replacement voucher for those who missed the passing mark.

Naturally, there is a limit, but the assurance that the training providers stand behind their instruction quality can offer some piece of mind to the potential workforce member.

Government Training

The Defense Cyber Investigations Training Academy (DCITA) is the training directorate of the Defense Cyber Crime Center (DC3). The DC3 is located in Maryland and the Air Force serves as the executive agent. The DCITA, serves a diversity of students from the DoD and many Federal agencies. From a modest beginning in 1998, the Academy has grown into a highly regarded cyber training institution offering more than 30 courses in five categories of specialization. Courses range from digital forensic investigation basics to collecting, preserving and examining digital media in a wartime environment. Delivered in modern classrooms and across leading-edge digital platforms, DCITA courses are designed to strengthen and test student capabilities in real-world scenarios. To participate, one must either be active duty, government civilian, assigned to a US Government agency or an official representative of a government that has an existing memorandum of understanding with the US Government for cyber training, or at the discretion of the DCITA director. A government Common Access Card (CAC) or other Federal token will be required to gain access.

The Federal Virtual Training Environment (FedVTE), initially developed and hosted by Carnegie Mellon but now hosted by the government, offers a variety of hands-on distance learning training opportunities. This is training location is also available to veterans who are looking to move into another career. Active duty and current government personnel can register by using their current government email, while veterans can register by providing proof of their status and registering. Recently, the Department of Homeland Security (DHS) has expanded access to FedVTE to state, local, tribal, and territorial (SLTT) government employees across the country.

The Defense Acquisition University (DAU) was established to provide a global learning environment to develop qualified acquisition, requirements and contingency professionals. They offer a course entitled "CLE 074 Cybersecurity Throughout DoD Acquisition." This specific continuous learning module provides foundational understanding of basic principles of cybersecurity and cybersecurity risk management in the defense acquisition field. This module is primarily intended for all DoD Acquisition career fields but especially military officers O-3 and above, civilians GS-9 and above, and industry equivalents across the defense acquisition workforce.

With the concern rising regarding operational technology (discussed earlier), the DHS established the **Industrial Control System Cyber Emergency Response Team** (ISC-CERT) to address the very unique and special actions to protect SCADA (supervisory control and data acquisition), ICS, and other operational technology. This on-line training provided through their virtual learning portal offers courses in various cybersecurity approaches to defend and secure industrial control systems. One does not have to be in government to get this training and can the website for more information and to register.

Commercial Training

Naturally there are plenty of commercially available training sources for those wishing to transition into the cybersecurity career field. As mentioned in the section on certification, *this does not constitute the list all of the potential commercial vendors that offer cybersecurity and related training.* The information provided comes from the organization's sites or literature and is provided for your benefit. Again, *this list no way constitutes an endorsement of those organizations specifically providing the certification.* There is no implied validation of the quality of the provider nor is the list in order of importance or value. These vendors all offer training and subsequent testing opportunities for most of the certifications listed in **Appendix C** as well as other training and certification options.

Founded in 1995 and headquartered in Cary, NC, **Global Knowledge** core IT training is focused on technology partners such as Amazon Web Services, Cisco, IBM, Microsoft, Red Hat, SAP and VMware. They also offer comprehensive professional development for advancements in application development, big data analytics, change management, cloud computing, cybersecurity and networking.

Started in 1997, **Ultimate Knowledge International** is an approved Pearson VUE and Prometric Testing Partner, which makes it convenient for their clients' IA and IT Workforce to schedule professional certification exams. They also offer a new Social Media Security Professional certification.

RPI is headquartered in Fredericksburg, VA with offices in Lexington Park, MD, Dahlgren, VA, San Diego, CA and Denver, CO. RPI brings together an agile and responsive team of national security, systems engineering and cyber experts. In addition to providing cybersecurity services, they also offer training and certification in a wide variety of options.

Learning Tree International, with headquarters in Reston, VA, offers a comprehensive selection of cybersecurity training and certification opportunities. As the others listed before, Learning Tree offers both on-site platform instruction, in a classroom or other facility, or they offer distance-learning opportunities.

Udemy is a relatively new construct – essentially an on-line marketplace – where an instructional location is provided for students to connect to independent contractor instructors, who provide live and recorded instruction, tutoring, and learning services in proprietary online classrooms. While the courses here can range from photography to programming, the opportunity to learn skills in HTML5, Java, Python, and Hadoop (just to name a few) is provided at a very competitive cost model.

Started just in 2015, **Cybrary IT, LLC** is another relatively new approach. Their stated goal is to provide the opportunity to learn cybersecurity, to anyone, anywhere, who wants that opportunity for free, forever. Costs to take this kind of training can be expensive; the founders noted that online learning has lower costs than classroom training. In coordination with current instructors, companies, and other institutions, they decided expand the "crowd-sourcing" model to offer the training for free, because this was the only way to give everyone in the world an opportunity to learn.

Certifications

You will find that the elements of the individual learning continuum in cybersecurity include your military training as a strong foundation you bring to the job in particular, your on-the-job experience in both what you did in the military and what you will do in the cybersecurity career, and your attitude towards continuous learning in which you are always studying and reading. What sets the cybersecurity career apart is the importance of the certifications you acquire, any academic degree programs in which you have or will participate, and any individual qualification programs you complete.

If it one thing that is well known in the cybersecurity career field, it's the number of potential certifications one can acquire. While it is always cautioned not to end up being a "cert chaser", recognizable as the individual with seven or eight different certification abbreviations after their name on their business card, it is strongly advised to gain some certified experience to show potential employers what skills you have. If one hasn't the formal education or degree, a recognizable certification is the next best thing. CIO magazine revealed that in a 2013 survey 85% of the respondents said that they hold a professional certification, and listed the Certified Information Systems Security Professional (CISSP), Cisco Certified Network Professional Security (CCNIP), and Certified Ethical Hacker (CEH) as the most popular credentials.[19]

Certifications are typically earned from a professional society and must be renewed periodically, or may be valid for a specific period of time. Certifications are one way for organizations to credential individuals with specific skill sets; they are portable, and do not rely on one company's definition of a certain job. They can enable workforce members to stand out as having necessary professional skills and provide an impartial, third-party endorsement of an individual's professional knowledge and experience.

Because you are coming from the military, you should be aware the DoD established a set of acceptable certifications (Figure 3.9) to gain entry into the cybersecurity workforce, and also listed some additional recommended certifications for those with more responsibilities. The DoD Instruction 8570, recently updated to DoD Instruction 8140, "[u]nifies the overall cyberspace workforce and establishes specific workforce elements (cyberspace effects, cybersecurity, and cyberspace IT) to align, manage and standardize cyberspace work roles, baseline qualifications, and training requirements."

There is strong movement at the time of writing this book where Federal agencies are looking to establish a more balanced "qualification" effort that can match the benefits of the "certification" approach. You may find that your Service may soon institute a qualification matrix that establishes some proficiency baselines. In this, we will see qualification processes develop that will

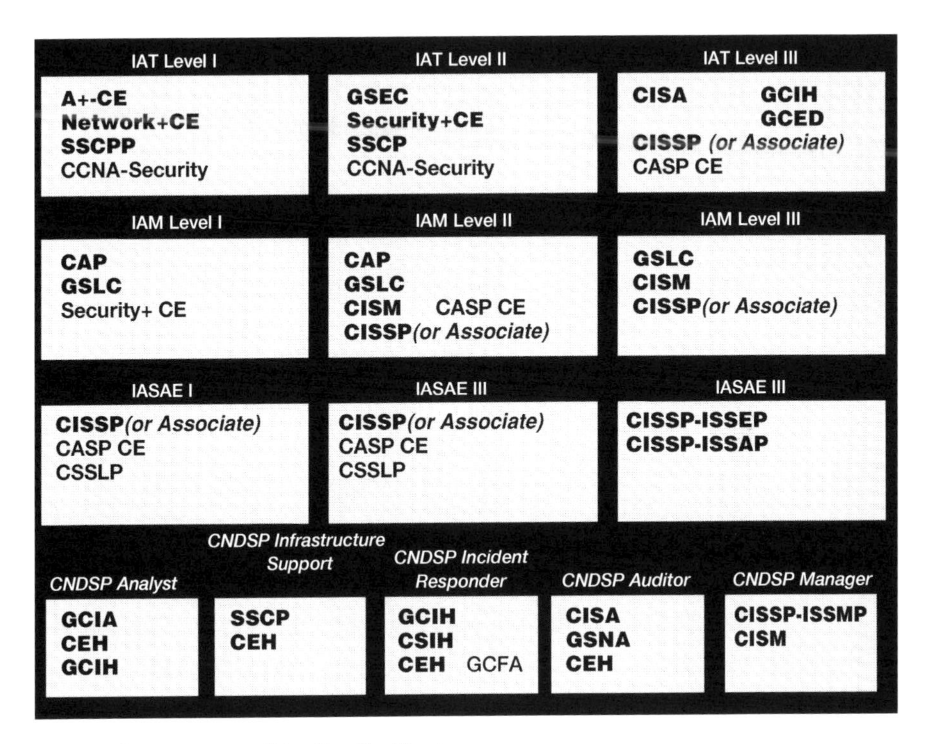

Figure 3.9 | DoD Approved Baseline Certifications

measure the ability of someone to perform a specific behavior (e.g., task, result, learning objective) to an established formal standard in order to demonstrate mastery of the behavior. As a consequence, cybersecurity personnel will have to follow an outlined training progression that supports continual skill development through individual and team proficiency. Another possible outcome is the government, and perhaps the rest of the potential employers, may find less and less need to rely solely upon certifications – especially with more junior members of the cybersecurity work force. In this book, we will address the topic of "certification" as implemented as of August 2016. (We did warn you that this is a dynamic field and changes are always happening!)

While the current recommended entry certification for those starting out in IT are those like CompTIA's A+ and Network+, individuals working in the cybersecurity field need to have certifications that are more cybersecurity focused, such as Security+. For more advanced responsibilities, the DoD recommended the (ISC)2 Certified Information System Security Professional (CISSP), the ISACA Certified Information Security Manager (CISM) or Certified Information Systems Auditor (CISA), or the SANS Global Information Assurance Certification (GIAC) Security Essentials (GSEC). In addition to these, the DoD wanted to see some type of certifications in the operating systems in which the individual would be working, i.e., Microsoft Certified Solutions Expert (MCSE), Red Hat Certified Technician (RHCT), or Cisco Cybersecurity Specialist (CCS), particularly a Cisco Certified Network Associate (CCNA)-Security. You can see more about how these certifications are acquired and maintained in **Appendix C.**

Lately the government, working through the NICE, is in the process of developing a list of applicable professional certifications. The certifications list that will be contained within the National Initiative for Cybersecurity Careers and Studies (NICCS) portal[20] will support the various government and contract support cybersecurity workforce frameworks, and will assist in building a technically adept, capable cadre of cybersecurity professionals to protect cyber infrastructure from foreign and domestic threats. In this way, service schools and professional military education centers will be able to provide training and skill enhancements in alignment with industrial certification, allowing government and military personnel to get the needed review and validation – meaning the government site will issue the tests and certificates in coordination with the industry testing body – without needed to pay for these privately. Sustainment costs, specifically the annual fees, would still need to be paid. As noted in Chapter Two, get access to your Service's COOL site for more information.

The list of various certifications and provisioning organizations in **Appendix C** is provided to help one prepare for the various roles and responsibilities in cybersecurity. Each section lists the certification, the issuing organization, a description of the certification, some requirements to obtain the certification, and a link to the certification site to provide more information. The first set of certifications are categorized as "information security certifications". Following that list is a section on "physical security and loss prevention", and the last list comprises a section on "audit certifications". All hyperlinks provided were verified as correct and active at the time of the writing of this chapter.

Naturally, *this does not constitute the list all of the potential certifications that can be obtained.* Some of these certifications have been industry staples for many years, while others are addressing new technologies or circumstances that have risen in the past few years. The information provided comes from the organization's sites or literature and is provided for your benefit. *Note: this list no way constitutes an endorsement of those organization specifically providing the certification. There is no implied validation of the quality of the certification or provider, nor is the list in order of importance or value.*

One should remember that in the process of acquiring a certification (or a set of certifications), there is an expectation of experience or background. The lack of either can make it more challenging for someone working to get into the field, but fortunately there are some alternatives. This is where the field offers a unique approach and that is through a variety of training and education programs.

There are also maintenance requirements for each and it is your responsibility to maintain your certification or recertify as required by the certification body. It is generally easier to maintain your certification through continuing education credits then retaking an exam. It's also cheaper, too. Many certifications charge an *annual maintenance fee.* Some companies and government organizations will offer to pay these fees as an employment benefit.

Continuing Professional Education (CPE) activities are dictated by the certification body but usually align to the certification domains. Certifications may also accept training outside of the core certification domains (e.g., management, writing, leadership, seminar participation, conference participation) as this reinforces the idea of a well-rounded and holistic professional. Certification bodies are generally liberal on what they will accept for credit; for example, online training classes or product demos are inexpensive methods of getting credit. See **Appendix C** for more information. Remember, though, it's ultimately your responsibility to maintain your certification!

Assessment #4 *(Skills)*

Figure 3.10 is the fourth assessment in the book and explores your personal preparedness for the cybersecurity career field. You may answer the questions here. When you are ready to analyze them, refer to Chapter 5. You can also use the companion guide to this book, available for download at GR8MilitaryCyber.com. Read each question and choose the correct answer for your current situation.

4: SKILLS	Strongly Disagree	Disagree	Neither Agree OR Disagree	Agree	Strongly Agree
I enjoy working in the cybersecurity career field.					
I have pursued an certification or degree in Information Technology and/or cybersecurity.					
I have performed IT and cybersecurity work in the past.					
I am comfortable working with networks, computer infrastructure, end user devices, hard ware, software, or programing.					
I have studied different occupations within the cybersecurity career fields with regard to personal interest.					
I have reviewed different types of cybersecurity certifications and analyzed the best certification for my situation.					
I desire to get an additional certification in an essential cybersecurity area, prior to departing the service.					
I enjoy working cybersecutiy functions and solving Information Technology					
I feel confident in my understanding of commercial cybersecurity and IT functions, services and operations.					
I enjoy the staying abreast of the changing the technological environment and cybersecurity issues within the IT industry.					

Figure 3.10 | Skills Assessment

Summary

Once comfortable with the cybersecurity career field, your career path, and your ability to articulate your skills to the commercial market, you will have a competitive advantage when transitioning from the military. The choice to prepare yourself to meet and excel at your post military IT career and enjoy the associated career benefits is yours to make. We encourage you to continue your education and learn all you can about IT and cybersecurity as a profession and to gain an awareness that transcends job titles, careers and industries.

Jeff Combs
Versatility

JEFF COMBS CAME INTO THE MARINE CORPS IN 1986 AND STARTED HIS MILITARY CAREER IN ARTILLERY. Injuries prevented him from reenlisting in that same MOS, and since he had attended DeVry Institute of Technology prior to his enlistment studying Computer Programming for Business Applications he took and passed the Electronic Data Processing (ELDP) test in early 1990 in order to lateral move into the 4034 Mainframe Computer Operator MOS.

His data communications career started with Jeff mounting tapes and pulling print for the first few months on 1st Shift. While pulling De-allocation reports for the production control unit, and reading the errors received due to invalid Job Control Language (JCL) statements used in execution, Jeff pointed out the errors and provided the proper commands to use to fix it from memory. Once his leadership found out he knew JCL, he was move to production control and promoted. Jeff was put in charge for the data center footprint design, maintenance, installation, power, and cooling for the mainframe associate processors and peripherals until Oct 1991 when he was sent to formal training for data control techniques and the 4038 MOS.

After tours in Okinawa, with DISA in St. Louis, with Headquarters Marine Corps (HQMC), and a tour in Quantico, the now SSgt Combs ended up in the Computer Network Defense (CND) section at the Marine Corps IT Network Operation Center (MITNOC) as the web risk assessment SNCOIC, encompassing the forensic technicians and initial vulnerability assessment cell capabilities.

Eventually now MSgt Combs served as the Vulnerability Assessment Lead for MITNOC (now the Marine Corps Network Operations and Security Center or MCNOSC) CND Section performing vulnerability assessments of Marine Corps Garrison and Tactical Network environments and enclaves supporting Joint Multi-disciplined Vulnerability Assessment (JMDVA) programs, Marine Corps Navy-Marine Corps Internet (NMCI) Cutover pre-assessments, and deployed network assistance to Operation Iraqi Freedom (OIF) in 2004 and 2006.

Retiring in 2007, Jeff entered private industry, but still supporting the Marine Corps in cybersecurity by working as a Certification & Accreditation (C&A) analyst for HQMC C4, then supporting the Marine Corps Operational Test and Evaluation Activity (MCOTEA) congressionally mandated Information Assurance and Interoperability (IA&IOP) Initiative as the Marine Corps Information Assurance Assessment Team (MCIAAT) Lead.

Jeff transitioned to a government civilian position in 2010 to work again for HQMC C4, and presently oversees the operational program for the DoD Cybersecurity Range and the Marine Corps Cyber Range in Stafford, VA. He has recently finished his master's work in computer science and is looking to begin his doctoral studies in the near future.

4

The Market Place

TREMENDOUS OPPORTUNITIES ABOUND FOR CYBERSECURITY PROFESSIONALS. The challenge is understanding and making an informed decision about where to conduct your job search. This very important decision needs to incorporate your comfort levels with risk, job satisfaction, security and growth. Learning about your desires as they relate to market place characteristics, will give you a distinct advantage in your job search decision. You may have already settled on a target job market. However, if you are unsure, look to this chapter to provide you with the tools to evaluate the pros and cons of your target market place.

Some transitioning personnel believe they will step into a great paying and interesting job for the rest of their life, immediately after leaving the service. However, this is not typical. Most of us change jobs, companies, and career fields many times. Learning the advantages and disadvantages of multiple transitions can better prepare you and your family.

> *"Opportunities multiply as they are seized."*
>
> **Sun Tzu 孫子**
> *The Art of War*

Opportunities after the military service for cybersecurity fall into roughly three sectors. These sectors are the focus of this chapter; civil service, government contracting, and commercial market place. While not a focus of this book, a brief discussion on Non-Profit Organizations (NPOs), and Federally Funded Research & Development Centers (FFRDCs) are presented as some service members choose this path after the service. For those that enjoy risk and working independently, entrepreneurship is a fourth option. There is a wealth of knowledge readily available on the entrepreneurship market. Entrepreneurship is not a focus as it is beyond the scope and objective of this book, but there are numerous examples where individuals with cybersecurity skills developed during their military time started their own company and have been successful. For those that enjoy risk and working independently, entrepreneurship will be covered briefly. There is a wealth of knowledge readily available on the entrepreneurship market. Like the non-profit organization, entrepreneurship is not a focus as it is beyond the scope and objective of this book. While this may appear to be a riskier approach to one's career, it remains an option to be considered.

Each market place is explored with regard to environment, opportunity, pay, and benefits as they relate to your interest and desires. Options and insights are offered so that you can weigh and consider all facets that impact you the most, from work/life balance to job benefits.

The market places are compared within the framework described above. A marketplace assessment is presented to further assist in identifying key factors while determining the best fit for you and your next position. As you read this chapter, note that the terms public sector, government, and civil service are all used interchangeably. Likewise, private sector, commercial company, and corporation are terms used in lieu of commercial market place. DoD Contracting is considered a hybrid to these distinct sectors.

Civil Service Market Place

The Federal government is the largest employment sector in the nation, hiring nearly 300,000 new employees every year. There are many government departments and agencies. All have many differences, from culture, professional opportunity, and employee satisfaction, and in some cases, pay scales.[1] Generally, civil service provides a tremendous opportunity for those desiring a stable work environment, great benefits and good pay. The reality is that people do not take civil service positions to get wealthy. In general, government workers want to use their skills and make a difference. Therefore, many choose civil service for these reasons, along with a growing number of transitioning military. "Most candidates interested in working for the government fully understand three clear benefits," said Evan Lesser, co-founder and director of ClearanceJobs.com, a secure website designed to match security-cleared job candidates with top defense industry employers. "First, is the issue of job security. Compared to contractors, Federal agencies are less subject to budget funding shortfalls and cancelled or re-bid contracts. Second, job seekers see a more structured promotion ladder. And third, working for the nation's largest employer means excellent health and retirement benefits."[2] If you are unaware, workers in commercial firms are three times more likely to be fired, compared to Federal employees. Civil service positions are generally more stable. This is comforting if stability is one of your most compelling decision factors.

Environment

The Partnership for Public Service (PPS), in concert with the audit and financial professional services firm Deloitte, annually publishes the "The Best Places to Work in the Federal Government". This cross agency assessment provides civil servant's opinions on workplace issues ranging from leadership, work-life balance, pay and personal ability for innovation.

John Palguta, PPS Vice President of Policy, stated "The reason people go to work for the government is because they want to do something meaningful and make a difference. Civil servants want to make good use of their skills and be engaged in mission accomplishment." The PPS assessment demonstrates civil servant personal job satisfaction and overall organization satisfaction.[3] An important factor making up organization satisfaction is pay. The last couple of years have been difficult for civil servant salary increases. Not surprisingly, recent reports show a significant categorical drop in satisfaction of Federal pay, due to the political and economic environment. Potentially due to fiscal concerns, there was also a decline in training and development opportunities, and rewards and advancement.[4]

Additionally, assessment results are broken into Federal agency size categories. Not surprisingly, the Departments of Navy, Air Force and Army are all listed and considered large agencies with 15,000 or more employees. Interestingly, for the civil servants interviewed, National Aeronautics and Space Administration finished on top with the highest satisfaction, and the DHS finished last. Figure 4.1 provides statistical results in overall job satisfaction for all Federal large agencies.[5] No sector receives a perfect score of 100, but the higher the score, indicates greater personal job satisfaction within that agency.

RANK	LARGE AGENCY (15,000 OR MORE EMPLOYEES)	SCORE
1	National Aeronautics and Space Administration	74
2	Department of Commerce	67.6
3	Intelligence Community	67.3
4	Department of State	65.6
5	Department of Justice	63.58
6	Social Security Administration	63
7	Department of Health and Human Services	61.9
8	Department of Transportation	60.9
9	Department of the Treasury	59.5
10	Environmental Protection Agency (tie)	59.3
10	Department of the Navy (tie)	59.3
12	Department of the Interior	58.9
13	Department of Veterans Affairs	57.3
14	Department of the Air Force	57.2
15	Office of the Secretary of Defense, Joint Staff, Defense Agencies	57
16	Department of Agriculture	56.1
17	Department of Labor (tie)	55.6
17	Department of the Army (tie)	55.6
19	Department of Homeland Security	46.8

Figure 4.1 | Statistical results for job satisfaction – Large Agency

Opportunity

Generally, civil service positions provide tremendous opportunities for military members in transition. The Federal government gives you an advantage due to your veteran status. Having served in a war, having a military connected disability or having served on active duty all give you an advantage and put you in different competitive categories. Therefore, your military service provides a significant benefit when competing for high quality civil-service positions.

When applying for civil service positions, you need to understand how the job announcement enables or precludes your advantageous veteran status. In many civil service applications, veteran status is awarded extra 'points' when identified by the applicant.

You may be eligible to compete under one or more categories designed for veterans such as Veterans' Recruitment Appointment (VRA), 30 Percent or more disabled veterans, and Veterans Employment Opportunities Act of 1998 (VEOA). These special hiring authorities for veterans give you a significant advantage if you are qualified. Figure 4.2 below summarizes these hiring authorities:

Remember, your competition when applying for these positions are current Federal employees with status and other United States citizens. Therefore, understanding your veteran eligibility is critical. Also, be aware that your eligibility does not make you qualified for the position.

Information on veterans transitioning to civil service:
www.fedshirevets.gov/hire/hm/shav/

In July of 2016, The Federal Cybersecurity Workforce strategy issued government wide actions to recruit, develop, retain, and sustain capable and competent cybersecurity workers. Now more than ever, if you decide to work as a civil servant in the cybersecurity career field, you may receive pay and benefits far greater than ever before. The Office of Personnel Management (OPM)

AUTHORITY	PROVISION	WHO IT APPLIES TO
VRA	VRA allows appointment of eligible Veterans up to the GS-11 or equivalent grade level.	Disabled Veterans; Veterans who served on active duty in the Armed Forces during a war declared by Congress, or in a campaign or expedition for which a campaign badge has been authorized; Veterans who, while serving on active duty in the Armed Forces, participated in a military operation for which the Armed Forces Service Medal (AFSM) was awarded Veterans separated from active duty within the past 3 years.
Excepted Service Cyber Security Workforce Schedule-A Hiring Authority	Services and Agencies can conduct direct hiring for GS-9 through 15 (or equivalent) in the following occupations: 0391 (Telecommunications); 0854 (Computer Engineer); 0855 (Electronic Engineer); 1515 (Operations Research Analyst); 1550 (Computer Scientist); and 2210 (IT Specialist) requiring cybersecurity skills and knowledg. Legislation and policy may also include additional specialty pay over and above the GS Rate.	Individuals who have verifiable experience in cyber risk and strategic analysis incident handling and malware/vulnerability analysis, program management, distributed control systems security, cyber incident response, cyber exercise facilitation and management, cyber vulnerability detection and assessment, network and systems engineering, enterprise architecture, intelligence analysis, investigation, investigative analysis and cyber related infrastructure inter-dependency analysis
30% Disabled	Enables a hiring manager to appoint an eligible candidate to any position for which he or she is qualified, without competition. Unlike the VRA, there is no grade-level limitation.	Disabled Veterans who were retired from active military service with a service-connected disability rating of 30 percent or more Disabled Veterans rated by the Department of Veterans Affairs (VA) as having a compensable service-connected disability of 30 percent or more.
VEOA	Gives preference eligible and certain eligible Veterans' access to jobs that otherwise only would have been available to status employees.	Preference eligible; and Service personnel separated after 3 or more years of continuous active service performed under honorable conditions.

Figure 4.2 | Civil Service Hiring Authorities for Veterans

established a program to assist Federal agencies with flexible compensation so they can recruit and hire highly skilled cybersecurity talent.

Just one example of these great new incentives for cybersecurity employees is the ability to have up to $60,000 student loans repaid by the Federal government. Other flexible compensations are focused on such areas as special pay, recruitment incentives, creditable service for annual leave accrual, relocation incentive, retention incentive and critical pay. You can read more about this "Compensation Flexibilities to Recruit and Retain Cybersecurity Professionals".[6]

Eligibility versus Qualification

The difference between eligibility and qualifications can be summed up as follows. Qualification is based solely on your knowledge, skills, and abilities (KSA's), and education, as discussed in chapters 2 and 3. Eligibility is meeting one or more criteria such as disabled veteran. A recent dimension in determining qualification for a job is the use of self-assessments, which are now becoming more of a standard than the exception. A series of questions are asked of the candidate during the application process to determine if you meet the KSAs for the position. Civil service hiring is also based on your capability to demonstrate your experience at the next lower level. So, if you are applying for a GS-12, your resume and questionnaire answers need to demonstrate your competencies and experience at the GS-11 level. Therefore, if you do not demonstrate your qualification for the position, your documentation will not be forwarded to the hiring official for review. Qualification for Federal workings in cybersecurity are outlined in Office of Personnel Management (OPM) General Schedule Qualification Standards. To review the specific KSAs for

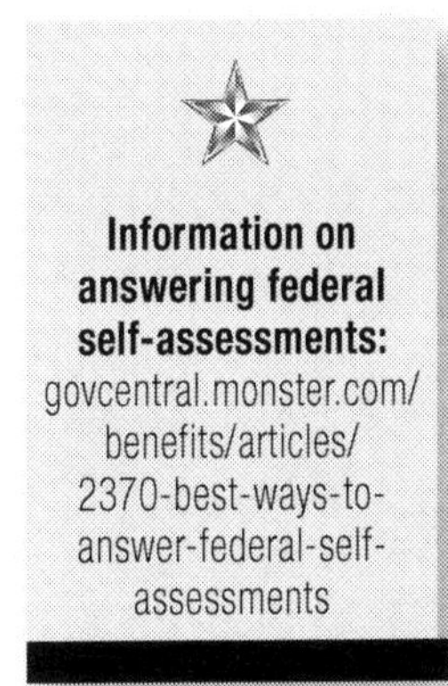

cybersecurity, look in the IT Management Series, 2210 (Alternative A).[7] Further information on answering Federal self-assessments can be found on *monster.com.*

Like other market places, there are significant advantages when it comes to mobility or being able to move to serve the needs of the government. When finding a position in a different locality you may receive pay for a move much like that in the military. Every position on USAJOBS.GOV will tell you if relocation is authorized. Sometimes, the department or the locality you are searching will offer relocation if it is hard to find someone with certain qualifications and/or interest in going to that particular location. For example, finding a job with relocation to the Washington D.C. area can be difficult. However, most rural locations without a significant local applicant pool will often provide relocation and/or financial incentive.

The best method for applying for civil service positions is through the comprehensive website "USAJOBS.GOV". This website not only posts jobs available by title description and location, it allows you to apply and track your application status. Helpful resume and application tips are given, enabling you to put your best foot forward.

Pay

Pay is a subject that is of great interest to all of us. Government Service (GS) pay scales operate on grade levels and geography. GS pay tables are standardized much like military pay tables, with the addition of locality pay adjustments.

In 2016, a GS-14 Cybersecurity Assessment Team lead in the Washington DC area can earn an annual salary of $108,887 to $141,555 depending on step. While in Salt Lake City, the same position pays from $99,785 to $129,723. An entry-level GS-12s Cybersecurity Analyst can earn $71,118 in Colorado Springs, and about $2,000 a year more in the Raleigh/Durham/Chapel Hill NC area. Therefore, you have to look at the correct scale for

the location for which you are applying. As an example, Tampa has no special "locality pay area" table. In the case where there is no scale for the metropolitan area you are considering, look at the scale called "Rest of United States". Figure 4.3 below delineates the GS Pay Scale for the Washington DC (24.78% locality payment) area.[8] Remember, no locality pay is given in overseas areas. Instead, overseas employees receive cost of living allowances (COLA).

SALARY TABLE 2016-DCB
INCORPORATING THE 1% GENERAL SCHEDULE INCREASE AND LOCALITY PAYMENT OF 24.78%
FOR THE LOCALITY PAY AREA OF WASHINGTON-BALTIMORE-ARLINGTON, DC-MD-VA-WV-PA
TOTAL INCREASE 1.46%
EFFECTIVE 2016

Annual Rates by Grade and Step

GRADE	STEP 1	STEP 2	STEP3	STEP 4
1	$22,888	$23,653	$24,414	$25,172
2	25,733	26,346	27,198	27,920
3	28,078	26,346	27,198	27,920
4	31,521	32,571	33,622	34,673
5	35,265	36,441	37,616	38,792
6	39,311	40,621	41,931	43,241

Figure 4.3 | Salary Table 2016 DC, showing locality pay for the Washington DC Area

Benefits

A tremendous number of benefits are available to civil servants. Benefits are organized into five major categories: benefits and insurance, leave and work-life balance, pay and savings, retirement, and personnel records. There is some variety between agencies, and the country's economy plays a great role in the availability of some benefits such as education. The major benefit categories are listed in Figure 4.4, but there are many benefits in each category. Remember, not all benefits are available from each department or agency.

HIGH LEVEL BENEFITS FOR CIVIL SERVANTS
Benefits and Insurance Programs
Leave and Work-Life Balance
Pay and Savings Plans
Retirement
Personnel Records

Figure 4.4 | Civil Service Benefits[9]

DoD Contracting Market Place

Many believe that the DoD contracting life blends the best of both attributes of GS and commercial market place while staying in a career supporting the military. The DoD contract environment is different from your military experience. You are still ultimately working for the defense of the nation, but you serve two masters. More importantly, the risk and rewards are both potentially greater than that of the civil service.

As a DoD contractor, you remain engaged with the defense of our nation. Many service members want to spend their post-military career doing something that feels familiar, and comfortable. This is why many pursue DoD contracting after military service. Transitioning to a DoD contracting position gives you comfort of a familiar language, and a grasp on the needs of the mission and organization.[10]

Environment

For many, DoD contracting is a very appealing post military career. In addition to potentially better wages for your work efforts than civil service, you have the potential to stay within the same department or agency you already know and understand while receiving significant flexibility not previously enjoyed. In most locations, you have the right to move on to another position or company should you become weary of your contract situation, boss' attitude, or government leadership. This knowledge and understanding provides relief for many in difficult or challenging situations.

Understanding the associated risks of DoD contracting is also very important. First, some find the government-contractor relationship challenging, especially after having been on the government side for a long period. If you choose to remain in the DoD environment, never loose site of the fact that the contractual relationship is adversarial by its very nature. There is goodness in this adversarial relationship. It is not only good for the taxpayer, but also provides constant checks and balances for both sides. The desire is to have a harmonious environment, with equilibrium between contract and performance. If either side gains the upper hand, then a difficult and challenging work environment will exist.

> *"One of the most important but difficult tasks in contract administration is to develop a proper working relationship. Cooperation between the parties is essential if the work is to be successfully performed, and yet the parties are, in a very real sense, adversaries. The Government often attempts to obtain performance within the contract price, while the contractor attempts to maximize profits either by doing the minimum acceptable work or by attempting to obtain price increase."* [11]

Why is this information important to you? Understanding the contract and government relationship is essential to your day-to-day life as a contractor. The question you face is how to deal with these types of relationship issues. Do you enjoy working through these types of challenges with contract leaders, program managers, and associated government counterparts? It is important to find the right fit. Learning to understand the challenges that lie ahead and being prepared to identify them, process them, and create optional courses of action will help you be successful. Challenges you might face as a DoD contractor include:

- One of the first things you will have to reconcile as a new contractor is that most contracts have an estimated date for completion. This proves challenging for most former military folks as your term of service was relatively guaranteed. How to deal with uncertainty of follow on work with your contract can be challenging and stressful. This is potentially the contractor's greatest anxiety. Not only does the contractor have to perform well, satisfy the customer, accomplish the tasks on time and to standard, but he or she must be keenly aware of the remaining contract duration and how well the contract at large is performing.

- If you desire a steady income, you may find coping with this risk difficult. The contractors that feel most comfortable with this arrangement will typically grow a sizable rainy day fund (2-3 months' salary) to assist during contract transitional periods. This risk mitigation strategy will provide some peace of mind, especially in these challenging economic and ever changing political times. Always remember, that even in a down economy, the government remains the largest single employer in the country and there are plenty of contracting jobs available, especially if you are willing to relocate.
- Another challenge to reconcile with is that you will be working with either a military or a civil servant government lead. They will have the final say on decisions. Constrained by rules and regulations, the Federal government is not famous for innovation or speed of bureaucratic consensus. These challenges may feel stifling or even frustrate some into choosing to move on to another occupation.

Opportunity

Like civil service, Federal contractors receive similar benefits with regard to mobility, future work and security. Contracts extend well beyond Washington D.C., with departments, agencies and offices around the world. That makes finding a job for those seeking a specific location, or desiring an opportunity to change localities, a great potential benefit. If you are mobile and good at what you do, the contract industry is going to have a job for you.[12] People move from job to job as contracts come and go. A DoD contracting career offers a significant chance for mobility and professional growth.[13]

Professional diversity is an added benefit of being a DoD contractor. As you acquire a variety of experience, you will be increasingly sought after. You will have a chance to move in and out of various professional experiences. If you are already an expert in one area, working different tasks and functions means you will have the chance to develop new skills and explore potential new specialized areas.

Finally, like civil service, your security clearance is invaluable if you choose to stay in DoD contracting. If your clearance re-investigation date has passed and you have lost your clearance, but you have the experience needed, many contractors will offer to recapture your clearance as part of your hiring package. Additionally, many Federal contractors will offer 'upgrades' of your clearance for required positions to meet certain contract requirements. You will not necessarily be reminded of your periodic investigation dates, so stay on top of your clearance. If a life event occurs such as financial issues, divorce, or arrest, make sure you inform your security officer quickly.

Job availability, good starting salaries and promotion potential are all positive aspects of contracting as long as you can go to where the jobs are. A defense contracting career is often the preference of many. If you have the skills wanted by the contractor at the right time, they will hire you on the spot with minimal paperwork and put you to work immediately. Further, you will have more control of your own destiny as your performance is the driving force in your career path. If you are performing, you will be promoted. If you are dissatisfied, then move to a more demanding job opportunity offering better pay.

Pay

As a contractor, you have a greater ability to negotiate a salary than your civil servant counter parts. As a company competes for new work with the government, a proposal is developed outlining various positions on the contract. The company will bid a specified price that takes into account a pay band for each position. Once awarded, the program manager has some flexibility within the pay band when hiring employees. This information may allow you to negotiate salary within the pay band for your desired position. Therefore, you will have to request a salary within a position's pay band, or you will probably not be hired.

As in the earlier quote from Sun Tzu, it is obvious the greatest road to success is to know yourself and know your environment. It is often said the first party to mention a figure during salary negotiation will not fare as well in the negotiation. Therefore, when questioned about your salary requirements, it is best to ask about the pay band for your position and request a well thought out number that resides within that pay band.

Benefits

First, know that human resource organizations will have specialists and experts that will explain and share current offerings in line with Federal and state laws. Generally, there is minimal variation between contract companies when it comes to benefit packages. Regardless of which Federal contractor you work for, you will find 100-150 hours offered as Paid Time Off (PTO) annually; or stated in military terms, leave. Of interest is that you accrue and take PTO by the hour and not by the day. This is helpful as you will need to take PTO occasionally for doctors' appointments, sick leave, or vacation. Unfortunately, most of the appointments that you are used to going to during a military duty day will have to be charged as PTO. Another option, if available, is flex time. Many companies desire that you get 40 hours of work in one week or 80 hours over a two-week period. Often, you can flex hours within the pay period so that you could work 42 hours one week and 38 the next. This type of arrangement varies by company. Regardless, just remember that the time cards are archived for inspection by the Defense Contract Audit Agency (DCAA). Therefore, contract and personal integrity are on the line and the time card must accurately reflect hours worked.

With regards to health benefits, most companies offer comprehensive healthcare where you pay a share and the company pays a share. If you are a retiree, some companies adjust your salary if you utilize your retiree healthcare benefit. Just know, if you desire to use a company's healthcare you can, but there will more than likely be a deduction from your pay check for the benefit. Vision and dental are a shared benefit as well. Just like your health insurance, if you are using TRICARE as an example, this benefit may not be of interest to you.

A flexible spending account is often available by larger companies in which you place some of your salary into an account for healthcare related expenditures. The dollars you place in this program reduce your taxable income, but must all be used for healthcare by the end of each year. Most companies, big and small will offer a 401(k) plan for long-term retirement savings. These plans will generally be matching funds up to about 3-5%. The company will determine which investment group you will be buying into and you will generally have a choice of funds. Some companies allow all your dollars to be fully "vested" upon your initial investment. Others will allow you to have their matching funds after a vesting period has surpassed (i.e., 50% vested after 2 years, 100% after 3 years). These vesting periods vary considerably between companies. Just remember that the 401(k) is for long-term retirement savings and significant penalties will normally be applied if you take out money prior to age 59½.[14] Additionally, some companies offer different types of stock options at discounted rates. This is an inexpensive way to invest in your company as you avoid brokerage fees in addition to any discount offered. Regardless, it is always recommended to place enough money in the 401(k) to get the matching funds, as you do not want to leave money on the table.

Larger companies have educational, training and certification assistance. Training authorization typically requires justification for the position you are in. Generally, companies will ask that you sign a document stating that you will not leave the company for some period of time (often 1 year) after taking the training dollars. This needs to be considered prior to taking training if you are thinking about changing companies, because some will hold back your last paycheck to pay for your training if you have not completed the allotted time.

If you have not surmised, bigger DoD contract companies generally offer bigger and better benefits. The alternative is that smaller companies may have greater salary and might be more attractive to employees desiring fewer benefits. Therefore, if benefits are not that important and more pay is a consideration, you may consider going to work for a smaller company. For example, if you have retiree benefits, you could negotiate more in salary. Finally, some small companies have greater flexibility for profit sharing with their employees. Regardless, weigh all of the benefits, salary, profit sharing and bonus capabilities to find the total compensation of the position. This exercise will assist you in weighing your options when comparing multiple job offers.

Commercial Market Place

Transitioning into the commercial market place from the military requires considerable risk tolerance and a high level of confidence in your ability to perform in a competitive environment. As mentioned at the beginning of this chapter, workers in commercial firms are three times more likely to be fired as compared to Federal employees. Working in the commercial market is not for the faint of heart, and the risks must be managed. However, most working in the commercial market quickly state that the rewards for this risk outweigh the job security of civil service.

Environment

Because workers strive for personal growth and reward, the commercial environment is often very competitive. In the commercial environment, employees generally try to remain competitive through innovation and providing business value to the organization. This determination and drive often requires numerous man-hours above and beyond a traditional 40-hour work week. Understandably, most workers join the commercial market place to earn significant amount of money, to be trained or gain experience, positioning themselves to earn significant money later.

It is always the desire in commercial market to achieve profitability and make money. Maximizing profit will drive all business decisions. If there are two choices, the best business case will be selected. Companies and managers will consistently pursue the highest potential profit at the best value every time they make a business decision. What this means to you as a potential worker in the commercial environment is that you must understand this concept and remain viable to the company, otherwise your services will not be needed for long. The profit concept is foreign to most public sector workers, including service members. Be advised, this concept sometimes becomes a bias against hiring veterans for some commercial hiring managers.

In high performing companies, there is tremendous focus on the bottom line. Managers desire to achieve this focus which leads to well understood, top to bottom goals and objectives. Two most important objectives driving decision making in the commercial market place are solution and price. Focusing on solution and price typically drives satisfaction and value in the commercial market. Managers must focus on providing and creating added value through the products and services offered by their company. The best solution is sought, as it increases return on investment and profit. Therefore, you need to be synchronized with management as you are held accountable for your work, and you are rewarded for success and potentially fired for failure.[15]

You need to understand what drives value in your work environment. Knowing this will help you align your day-to-day work effort as you deal with the customer as well as connect better when looking for a job. Nothing is more nerve racking than going to an interview or giving a presentation and not understanding how your employer perceives or derives value. Further, you are far better off talking to your leadership about their view regarding the best solution and profit, rather than unfinanced requirements and perceived cost savings which do not aid the organization's bottom line.

Opportunity

The commercial sector is set apart from the public sector with regard to rapid personal growth potential for achievers with financial reward and the promise of a creative and innovative environment. Rapid change is pervasive with the ever-changing business environment, and you will be rewarded if you embrace and become part of the change. One of the great attributes associated with the commercial market place is that your high performance will enable you to progress quickly without regard to a pay scale or longevity. As you work on your professional goals and career path, utilize opportunities to gain additional and diverse experience. Seek out ways to gain internal qualifications through training that aligns with your career goals. Keep in mind where you want to be and take on challenges to posture yourself for future success.

Financial reward is based largely on your ability to remain viable and valuable to the organizations. If you are adding to the bottom line you will be rewarded financially. The company rewards your positive impact and participation because if you move on, it may lose profit and key knowledge to the competition.

Innovation and creativity are also well rewarded in the private sector, as long as the innovation aids to the company's competitiveness, market position, or bottom line.

Remember, to remain competitive, companies will seek innovative workers and it will make change based on the business environment. If you like an exciting and dynamic environment, the commercial sector is for you.

Pay

Conventional wisdom has it that you'll always make more money in the commercial market place, with lower pay being the trade-off for job security in the Federal government.

That's generally true. The Federal Salary Council, a group of union officials and pay policy experts, says Federal workers overall earn about 35 percent less than their commercial-sector peers.[16]

Another aspect to remember is that your cybersecurity experience from the military, if understood by your hiring manager, will assist in landing a good paying job. Cybersecurity professionals report an average salary of $116,000, or approximately $55.77 per hour. That's nearly three times the national median income for full-time wage and salary workers, according to the Bureau of Labor Statistics. But it's more than just the money. Cybersecurity professionals say that they actively seek employers with strong reputations for integrity and those that are recognized as leaders in their field.

Benefits

In general, benefits are similar or better than DoD contracting. The one exception is small business may provide you fewer benefits. That being said, small businesses must offer the following benefits as they are considered mandatory by the federal government.[17]

- Social Security Credit
- Unemployment Insurance
- Workers Compensation
- Minimum Wage
- Overtime Pay

Surprisingly, the following benefits are not required to be given to employees and you may see a variation of these benefits at every company.

- Retirement plans
- Health plans (most employers are still working through the sort out the Affordable Care Act)
- Dental or vision plans
- Life insurance plans
- Paid vacations, holidays or sick leave

Having said all of this, most large companies offer tremendous benefits and some unexpected surprises upon arrival. Price Waterhouse Coopers (PWC)[18] advertises the following "Perks" on their website:

- **Sabbatical:** Employees can take four-week sabbaticals with 20 percent to 50 percent of pay.
- **Tuition Reimbursement and Scholarships:** Employees can get up to $5,250 in financial assistance to further their education.
- **401(k):** PWC contributes 5 percent of an employees' annual pay to their 401(k) retirement savings plans even if they don't make their own contribution.

- **Volunteer Hours:** Every employee receives 10 hours per year of paid time off to volunteer for charities of their choice.
- **Rewards and Recognitions:** Employees can earn contribution awards when managers or partners recognize them for excellence, outstanding effort and teamwork.

Non-Profit Organizations - FFRDC/UARC

A Nonprofit Organization (NPO) functions with a purpose or function, other than making a profit. NPOs are typically dedicated to furthering a particular social cause or advocating ideals.

FFRDCs are unique nonprofit entities sponsored and funded by the U.S. government. The Federal Acquisition Regulation (FAR) requires they operate in the public interest free from organizational conflicts of interest and can therefore assist in ways that industry contractors cannot. FFRDCs assist with governmental scientific research and analysis, systems development, and systems acquisition. FFRDCs operate in the industries of defense, homeland security, energy, aviation, space, health and human services, and tax administration. FFRDCs are grouped into three categories focusing on different types of activities:

- System Engineering and Integration Centers
- Study and Analysis Centers
- Research and Development Centers (includes national laboratories)

FFRDCs were established to provide the DoD with unique analytical, engineering, and research capabilities in many areas where the government cannot attract and retain personnel in sufficient depth and numbers. Currently, there are over 40 recognized FFRDCs sponsored by the U.S. government. UARC are strategic DoD research centers associated with one or more universities.

Regardless, all NPOs need cybersecurity support. If a small NPO, this support may be outsourced. If it is a large NPO, this may be a lucrative location for your job search. If you decide to go this route, an NPO wants to know that you are truly interested in their cause and what they are doing – just as much as the skills that you have. You may show your loyalty to the cause and your interest by starting out with the organization as a volunteer.

Entrepreneurship

As mentioned earlier in the chapter, the subject of entrepreneurship is only lightly discussed. There are many resources available for this sector as there are many variations of start-up businesses. For example, you might want to start a cybersecurity consulting firm as a disabled veteran or minority owned business.

Regardless, each city/county/state offers a variety of classes and seminars on how to successfully start these types of companies. If you should try entrepreneurship as a consultant or business, keep in mind the following concepts:

- You must be willing to take on risk to achieve success.
- There is no cookbook and you cannot be a quitter.
- You need to have deep pockets or backing
- You need to understand the business, tax and government laws, contracting associated with the business you are going pursuing
- The measure of success for entrepreneurship survivability is 5 to 10 years out.
- Entrepreneurship is tough on the family and quality of life, unless there are other sources of income
- You must be an optimist and pride yourself on doing things differently.

Market Place Comparison

Understanding how the commercial market place differs from the government is absolutely essential for your success in transitioning from the military. Knowing the value proposition is essential. Public organizations will perceive value through mission accomplishment with the least amount of hassle or disturbance. Private organizations will find value through seeking out the least cost and greatest capability, thereby enhancing the bottom line.

When looking at this question from the employee perspective, a term coined in England when comparing the public and private market place is "Sector Envy". Universally, it appears that the "Grass is always greener" when looking at the opposing market place. With wildly varying risks, rewards, salaries, benefits, and job security, "Sector Envy" is a very appropriate term among American workers as well. Let's compare the public and private market place as they relate to your personal desires.

With regard to "Sector Envy" it is interesting to note that there is an increase in the migration of workers moving back and forth between government agencies, DoD contractors and the commercial market place. Employees with contracting backgrounds make easy transitions into Federal and civil servant jobs due to their knowledge, skills and abilities. Generally, as a former service member becomes more familiar with commercial certifications and the new environment, they become more marketable in the commercial market place. Know that many have come before you and not only changed jobs, but also market places on multiple occasions.

So what do you need to know? You should be aware that there are many factors that separate public and private sectors. Fundamental environmental factors include: value proposition, business case, turnover challenges, and measures of success. Obvious factors are financial rewards, job security, benefits, and your ability to easily transition from the Service. Some of the not so obvious factors are work-life balance, changing work environment, workload and career ladder. A few comparative environmental factors are given below:

Value proposition - Private sector managers worry about creating added value, while public-sector managers are often stifled by outdated, restrictive laws, regulations and policies that prevent rapid change or action.

Business case - In private industry there are clear well understood top to bottom goals and objectives. In the public sector goals are often divergent or disparate and can lead to confusion.

Turnover challenges - In government, leaders are often rotated in and out to ensure proper grooming and development of leadership. This thrash of leadership creates potential organizational change based on personality rather than achieving unity of movement towards goals and objectives. The corollary in the business world is a business merger or hostile takeover.

Key Performance Indicators (KPI) – In the absence of clearly understood business goals, government often invents measures of success that might be more aligned to short-term contractual and personal goals versus long-term business goals.

Stone walling – In the government setting, if a leader is not well-received, senior civil servants will slow roll and wait out leadership change. This is especially true for political appointees or temporary military leadership. In the private sector there is no business case for this type of activity, as most companies will find this unacceptable.

These fundamental factors have huge environmental implications on workplace satisfaction. Figure 4.6 below compares positive responses from Federal government employees against commercial-sector workers. These questions reflect the impact of some environmental factors previously discussed. The results show the public sector holds a slight edge over the commercial market place when employees are asked if they like the kind of work they do.[19] However, when it comes to recognition, training and supervisors, the commercial market place employees are a big winner.

QUESTION	GOVERNMENT-WIDE	COMMERCIAL MARKET PLACE	GAP
I like the kind of work I do.	81.2	75.0	6.2
My work gives me a feeling of personal accomplishment.	69.7	70.0	-0.3
I have enough information to do my job well.	69.3	71.0	-1.7
The people I work with cooperate to get the job done.	72.3	78.0	-5.7
I am given a real opportunity to improve my skills in my organization.	59.6	66.0	-6.4
Overall, how good a job do you feel is being done by your immediate supervisor/team leader?	65.8	73.0	-7.2
How satisfied are you with your opportunity to get a better job in your organization?	31.5	44.0	-12.5
How satisfied are you with the training you receive for your present job?	46.6	61.0	-14.4
How satisfied are you with the information you receive from management on what's going on in your organization?	44.8	60.0	-15.2
How satisfied are you with the recognition you receive for doing a good job?	42.6	64.0	-21.4

Figure 4.6 | Comparison - Federal to Commercial work satisfaction

Personal Market Place Satisfaction

Having read the environmental factors, a side-by-side market place satisfaction scale is presented for your understanding of the remaining factor differences. When looking at the market places for future opportunities, it is beneficial to optimize where you search. Most of us do not have the latitude of time on our side to look for and, more importantly get a job. You can spend months searching through the job listings. We spend much of our lives at work, and it is worth being happy during that time. Additionally, about 20% of people leave their jobs every year, according to the Bureau of Labor Statistics.

If it is important for you not to be part of the statistic and continually rotate jobs, there are a few items to consider. A key consideration to staying in a particular job is your personal satisfaction. Sometimes we forget the "personal satisfaction" factor, as this will increase the chances of remaining in the same position. Make an honest evaluation and list the factors necessary for your workdays to be as enjoyable and rewarding as possible.

Nine satisfaction elements are utilized in the personal satisfaction scale. The definition of each element used in this tool is defined below in Figure 4.7.

ELEMENT	DEFINITION
Creative Environment	Opportunity/need to be creative in the job.
Financial Reward	Probability of salary increase and bonus based on success.
Change	Frequency of change expected on the job to maintain position.
Workload	Level of work expected to perform on the job to sustain position.
Career Ladder	Clearly defined job growth expectations and requirements.
Education Reimbursement	Financial reimbursement for additional education and certification.
Work/Life Balance	Based on rules and work week expectations, presents a level of work/life balance important to keep personnel satisfied.
Job Risk	Volatility and chance of losing your job due to issues outside of your control.
Benefits	Level of standardized benefits to include medical/dental, savings, retirement, vacation time, education, etc.

Figure 4.7 | Factor Definitions

To assist in your organization of these personal satisfaction elements, the following market place satisfaction scale is presented. Columns represent the four market places covered in this chapter: civil service, DoD contractor, commercial, and entrepreneur. Rows represent typical elements as they relate to the market place. The scale is presented below in Figure 4-8. Probabilities are plotted for each factor in each marketplace based upon whether the element has a high-medium-low likelihood of influence in the marketplace. Data for the grid is based upon years of discussion and experience. There will always be exceptions, but for your purposes, the table should prove helpful to those in transition from the military, offering a foundation that can be customized based upon your own experiences.

At a glance, two items that might be of importance to you are security and WLB. If these two are important to you, you may gravitate towards the civil service work. If you enjoy risk and desire a highly competitive and potentially creative environment, you may align yourself with commercial industry, or perhaps, even entrepreneurship.

When considering all the elements of the table, you will notice that the civil service marketplace offers more stability and you can have relative confidence that you will be able to remain in the position, with a standard offering of benefits, salary and a pro-active WLB. If you desire to climb the corporate ladder and create an opportunity of accelerated promotions and desire to try to capture a better than average salary due to your creative mindset, you will be better served in either the commercial of entrepreneurial markets.

Finally, the scale roughly correlates with personality types. You may have previously identified with either 'Type A' or 'Type B' behaviors. 'Type A' personalities are typically ambitious, rigidly organized, high achieving, "workaholics", multi-taskers, highly motivated, insist on deadlines, and hate both delays and ambivalence. Contrastingly, 'Type B' personalities live at a lower stress level and typically work steadily, enjoying achievement but do not become stressed if immediate gratification is not present. They may be creative and enjoy exploring ideas and concepts and are often reflective.

Use Figure 4.8 to assist you in developing thoughts on which market place may provide the best landing space for you after the service based on your personality and style. Take a few moments and ponder the difference to ensure you are pursuing the best match for your lifestyle.

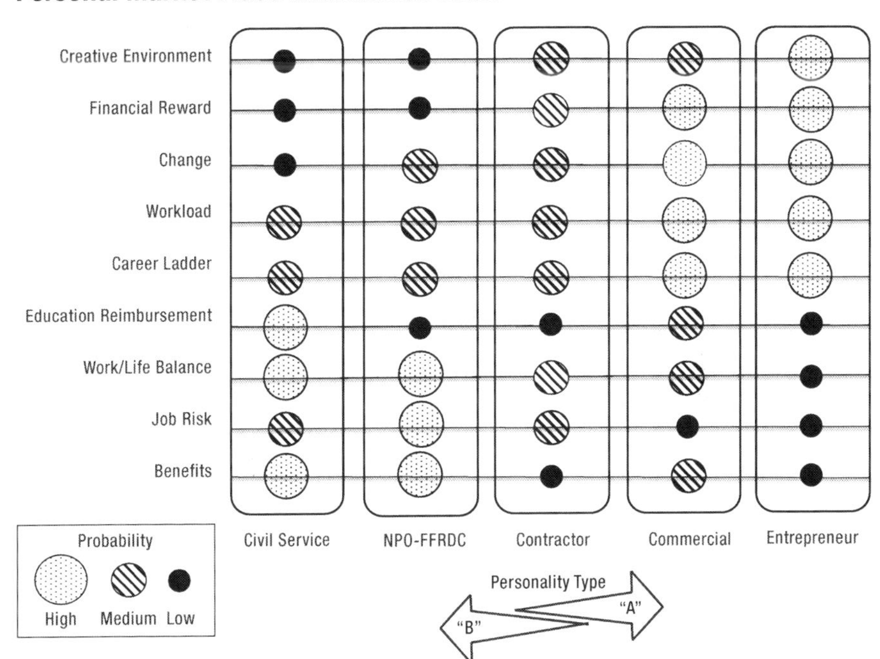

Figure 4.8 | Personal Market Place Satisfaction

Assessment #5 *(Market Place)*

Figure 4.9 is the fifth and final assessment in the book, exploring personal factors that influence which market place offers the best alignment to your interests. You may answer the assessment questions here. When you are ready to analyze them, refer to Chapter 5. You can also utilize the companion guide to this book, available for download and print out on-line at Gr8MilitaryCyber.com. Read each question and choose the correct answer for your current situation.

5: MARKET PLACE	Strongly Disagree	Disagree	Neither Agree OR Disagree	Agree	Strongly Agree
Potential salary increase is more important to me than job security.					
A potentially stressful work place and long hours are not concerns for me.					
Creativity and innovation are more important than procedures.					
I am excited by the prospect of leaving public service and trying something different in the private sector.					
I desire promotions based on personal performance rather than on pay scales and longevity.					
Switching companies or changing positions frequently are not concerns for me.					
Feeling safe from competition and losing my job are factors I rarely think about.					
I desire to work in an environment that rewards my innovative behavior and 'out of the box' thinking.					
An environment where I can share and use my military experiences and knowledge is not overly important to me.					
I prefer driving or "making" my career path rather than waiting on promotion.					

Figure 4.9 | Market Place Assessment

Summary

Once comfortable with the basics, knowledge of the market place will help you gain a competitive advantage and keep you from proceeding down the wrong path for your next career. A few departing thoughts are presented as you progress in your job search and transition:

1. If you have a target market place in mind, make sure your resume is tailored to the markets you desire and that your network and connections will be able to assist.

2. You can inquire and ask questions at the end of an interview such as how the company views different positions; how risk adverse the company is; how mature their documentation processes are; what tools are used; what career path options are open to someone starting in your position and what criteria is used to measure and advance.

3. Once at the job, think out-of-the-box. Do not just go into the job and expect a list of daily activities to perform. In the military, you had to adapt. Now is the time to utilize that trait.

4. Gain confidence in the new position by understanding both the official and unofficial political fabric of your environment.

5. Understand your peers and your boss(es). As you master your expected job skills, continue to branch out as far as possible to other divisions, groups, and teams. This knowledge will increase your overall understanding and appreciation of the organization, as a holistic view will assist you in evaluating the position you are in and how valid it connects with your expectations and goals.

The choice to prepare yourself and perform good market place selection, is yours to make. You are encouraged to continue to grow your understanding of these different sectors. In the story below, discover how one woman, who was given information assurance as a 'side' duty in the Army, built her knowledge base and launched a career in cybersecurity through the civil service.

You too will find your experiences invaluable as you make your transition.

Darcy Hotchkiss
Determination

DARCY HOTCHKISS ALWAYS HAD AN INTEREST IN THE MILITARY FROM YOUNG AGE. The idea of service and being a part of something import that was much bigger than her and the camaraderie was very appealing. At the point in her life when she started to look seriously at joining, she was a single mom, finishing high school in night school, and was trying to work and go to college at the same time. She was living in a paper mill town with a slow economy in central Maine, on welfare, and living in public housing. It was a long and difficult road ahead and she couldn't see where her life was going for either her or for her daughter's future. She made the decision to join the Army because she wanted more options for both of them, and she knew that being in the Army would give her experience and education that would serve as a stepping stone for what she would do for the rest of my life.

She decided to transition from the military to the civilian sector because she was looking at the diversity of opportunities available as a civilian in the IA program manager roles that were leading most of the cybersecurity and accreditation efforts of that time. She weighed the options of staying in the military longer, but, at that time cyber was not a career billet in for active duty and she really intended to be on that career path.

Initially, she was handed the information assurance /cyber duties as an additional duty. It was before cybersecurity was popular, and at that times wasn't taken serious or wasn't well considered by leadership. It was often seen as additional duties to submit paperwork and was seen as a bureaucratic paper drill that bogged down a communicator's ability to work in the more traditional communication fields. She spent time reading the policies and guidance and trying to understand the processes and documentation required to make everything work smoothly. As the lower enlisted personnel in charge of the processes she quickly became the subject matter expert. From there she saw other opportunities to take on bigger and more challenging roles in the various domains of cyber.

The military armed her with leadership skills, professionalism and the ability to adapt and overcome adversity. Cybersecurity, when in a position of leadership, can be confrontational especially when having to make unpopular decisions or recommendations. She discovered how to leverage the ability to lead in the face of adversity, and make fact-based analysis in high pressure real world scenarios. The biggest lesson she learned in the military is that good leadership is critical to the success of any sized project or effort. She also learned that you don't have to know all the details or how it's all going to go in order to begin a project. The most import part of success professionally is beginning with knowing your desired end state and then moving forward with that in mind first.

Because of her expertise and time working in the cyber realm, she decided to pursue and target university studies toward business management. She felt that getting a cyber or engineering degree would pigeon hole her into just technical roles and professionally, plus she wanted to move to the executive business management opportunities. She still seeks opportunities to take industry cybersecurity certifications and courses in order to keep her CISSP credential relevant and also to stay abreast of new technologies and advanced persistent threats (APT).

5

The Right Fit

NOW IT IS YOUR TURN.

While reading this book you have gained focus of your strengths, simultaneously learning about the job market and the cybersecurity profession. You have the logic behind positioning yourself for the job market and you have gained the confidence to attack the competition. Now you will organize these elements together to shift your mental posture from the defensive to the offensive.

Combining the knowledge gained from this book with the personal information you collected through the assessments will facilitate the creation of a high impact personal strategic roadmap. This exciting instrument provides directed self-awareness while gaining an

> *"You have brains in your head. You have feet in your shoes. You can steer yourself any direction you choose. You're on your own. And you know what you know. And YOU are the one who'll decide where to go..."*
>
> ~ Dr. Seuss,
> Oh, The Places You'll Go!

understanding of your strengths and the confidence required taking on the next challenge.

Several tools are introduced in this chapter. The first tool is for the charting of your assessment scores collected in earlier chapters. This tool identifies those personal areas that can be exploited (strengths) and those areas for possible improvement. The second tool is the personal strategic roadmap. Assessment scores that reflect areas for possible improvement will be transferred onto your personal strategic roadmap. This roadmap will be used continuously as you track, monitor, and achieve your personal goals.

To gain the best results, work through the process with honest introspection and reflection. Completing these steps enable your preference for market place, career and level of readiness for transitioning into the cybersecurity profession. There are three steps involved:

1. Gaining an understanding and control of personal information and capabilities that you have, thereby reducing risks of the unknown.
2. Analyzing outcomes of each assessment to identify what you already possess in your "kit bag" for successful resume writing, interviewing, and transition.
3. Setting goals based on those areas you choose for improvement. These improvements are to be charted, monitored, and tracked on the personal strategic roadmap until they are achieved.

Step One - Gaining Control of Your Personal Information (The UNK-UNK Chart)

In certain areas of the military and commercial world, the UNK-UNK chart is used to depict information available about organizations. The title of the UNK-UNK chart is derived from using "UNK" as an abbreviation to "Unknown". The chart is useful not only to military planning and operation groups, but to commercial organizations performing risk analysis. When you transform an organizational construct to a personal perspective, the UNK-UNK chart is useful in identifying and understanding what you know and don't know about yourself.

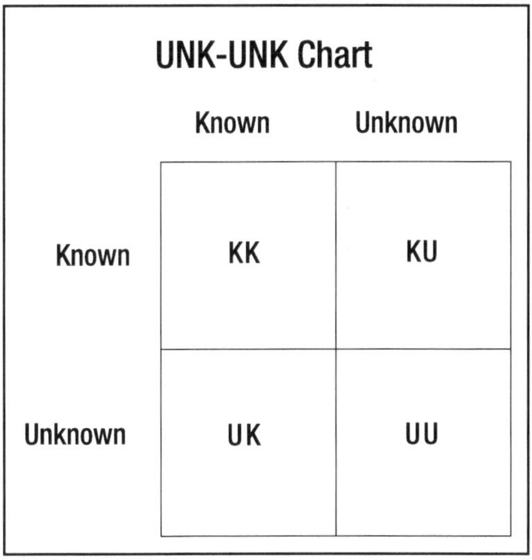

The UNK-UNK chart is broken into four quadrants (Figure 5.1). Quadrants are defined with regard to the terms "Known" and "Unknown". These terms refer to a general understanding of information an organization has awareness of ("knowns") and information not known ("unknowns"). When you array these two terms on both sides of the chart and step through the following analysis, an approach to reducing your "unknowns" begins to unfold. Organizations categorize information as follows: What information they know (KK); what they know that they don't know (KU); what they do not know that they know (UK); and, what information they do not know exists and are completely unaware of (UU).

UNK-UNK Chart

	Known	Unknown
Known	KK	KU
Unknown	UK	UU

Figure 5.1 | UNK-UNK Chart

The upper left quadrant (KK-information you know you know) is a very valuable commodity. In this quadrant, the organization is "self-aware" and this knowledge can be exploited. By way of a military example, if you know you know the location of the enemy, you plan and move to contact to destroy the enemy at this location. Similarly, in business, a corporation would want to try to exploit its capabilities in the marketplace if they knew they had a competitive advantage. From a personal perspective, your skills, characteristics, abilities, and sense for the type of marketplace you want to pursue are very valuable. Acknowledge and exploit this information on your resume and during your interviews to achieve the best career alignment.

The upper right quadrant (KU, or, know what you do not know) denotes an organization, which understands they do not have certain information elements needed for success. Capturing these information elements provides tremendous value for study, assessment and improvement within the organization. For example, if a company does not have market information they consider valuable, they work to resolve the information shortfall in an effort to gain a competitive advantage. From a personal perspective, knowing that you do not have a capability is of vital importance. During an interview, not knowing the hiring manager's expectations and how the organization perceives value can bring the interview process to a halt. Take some time to know the customer to try and reduce the risk associated with this quadrant. KU elements become goals for your personal strategic roadmap. Achieving these associated goals turn KUs into KKs, increasing your competitive edge.

The bottom left quadrants (UK, or, you don't know what you know), is very harmful in combat. To avoid this outcome, military organizations employ a term or slogan "Who else needs to know?" When critical information is not shared, it can cause mission failure. A company may know they have a capability, but fail to see its value or how to exploit the capability, and their competitor gets to market faster. Applying this quadrant to your personal transition, you want to ensure you have uncovered your capabilities, even the ones that you do not expect to be of significant marketability. During interviews, take time to exploit and share your accomplishments, certifications, and experiences as they relate to the company.

Finally, the bottom right quadrant (UU, or information you don't know that you don't know) is all about reaction. "Ignorance is bliss" is a common cliché associated with this quadrant. In this quadrant, action occurs and change happens rapidly if you do not have the information necessary for counter-action. It is the riskiest of quadrants as there are unex-

> ***"One defends when his strength is inadequate; he attacks when it is abundant."***
>
> **Sun Tzu 孫子**
> ***The Art of War***

pected outcomes, because you could not anticipate events. In the corporate world, while you continue the status quo, your competitor may develop something viable and exploit the market opportunity before you ever realize what happened!

Why go through the exercise of analyzing the UNK-UNK chart? Your objective is to reduce the size of any unknowns and associated risks. As shown in Figure 5.2, reducing the level of "unexpected unknowns" and turning them into "knowns" is the best method to increase your personal edge and confidence. There will always be "unknown" shortcomings, but it is essential to reduce the 'unknown' quadrant as much as possible by expanding other quadrants, making your 'known' area as large as possible. For this to happen, reflect upon your undiscovered skills and characteristics.

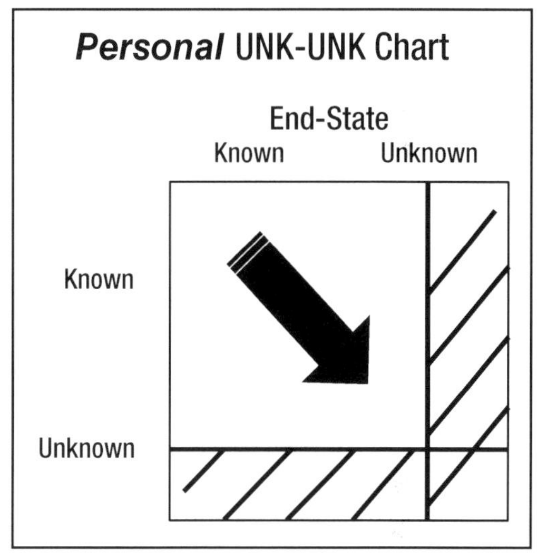

Figure 5.2 | Competitive Gain

With the knowledge of the UNK-UNK chart, let us use the remaining tools of this book to help you determine what areas you need to exploit and what you need to improve upon.

Step Two - Understanding Assessment Results

Analyzing assessment outcomes assists in determining what you already have in your "kit bag" for transitional success. In each prior chapter, assessments were provided in five key transitional areas, summarized in Figure 5.3 below. As mentioned in the introduction, your assessment results should have been documented in the gem formats, available through the free downloadable companion guide found at Gr8MilitaryCyber.com.

Assessment Type	Chapter	Topic Areas
Personal Characteristics	2	Leadership, motivation, creativity, managing others, personal growth, organizational skills, repeatability, working with others, visionary
Environment	2	Family, re-locations, financial obligations, retirement objectives, schools, faith, etc.
Timing	2	Service goals met, training/certification goals, time remaining, commitment, financial preparedness
Skills	3	Military skills, educations, certifications, credentials, jobs
Market Place	4	Civil Service, contractor (DoD), commercial market place, analysis based on income, stress, competitiveness, predictability, longevity, mental growth, benefits

Figure 5.3 | Assessment Topics

Star Charting

To assess your strengths and improvement areas, a chart in the form of a star will be created utilizing the companion guide. Begin building the star by charting each assessment score on a 'gem' (Figure 5.4) on the y-axis. The y-axis represents your readiness to transition; or how 'ready' you are to transition from the military. For each assessment, use the question number and plot answer results on the gem axis. It is highly recommended that you use the free companion guide for the assessment. However, the five gems and the star can be manually recreated.

When plotting the results of your assessments, you will likely find more than one answer on an axis point. Simply cluster the plotted points. Analysis of each assessment gem offers a journey to unfolding your personal roadmap. In turn, the roadmap will guide you to the best-suited career path in the best-suited market place.

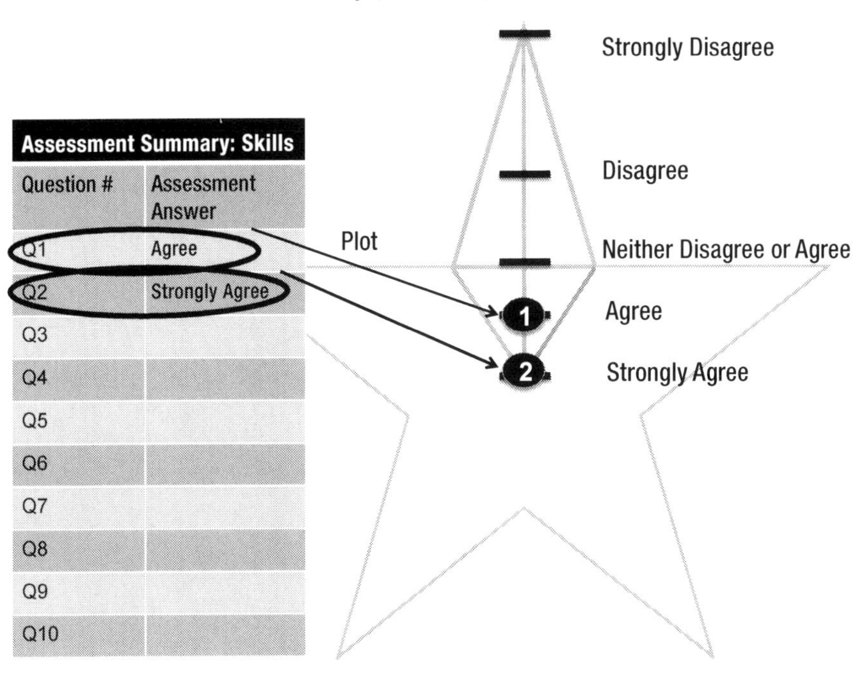

Figure 5.4 | Star Chart Mapping

Once each gem is completed, combine all gems with the associated assessment results to build the star chart provided in the companion guide to view your aggregate results (Figure 5.5). When combined, these plotted assessment results form the shape of a star, resulting in a personal index. Your personal index summarizes key indicators from your personal, environmental, timing, marketplace and skills assessments; clearly stating your readiness, marketplace, and ease of transition from the military. With this knowledge you will understand the best options to pursue, given your strategy goals and objectives.

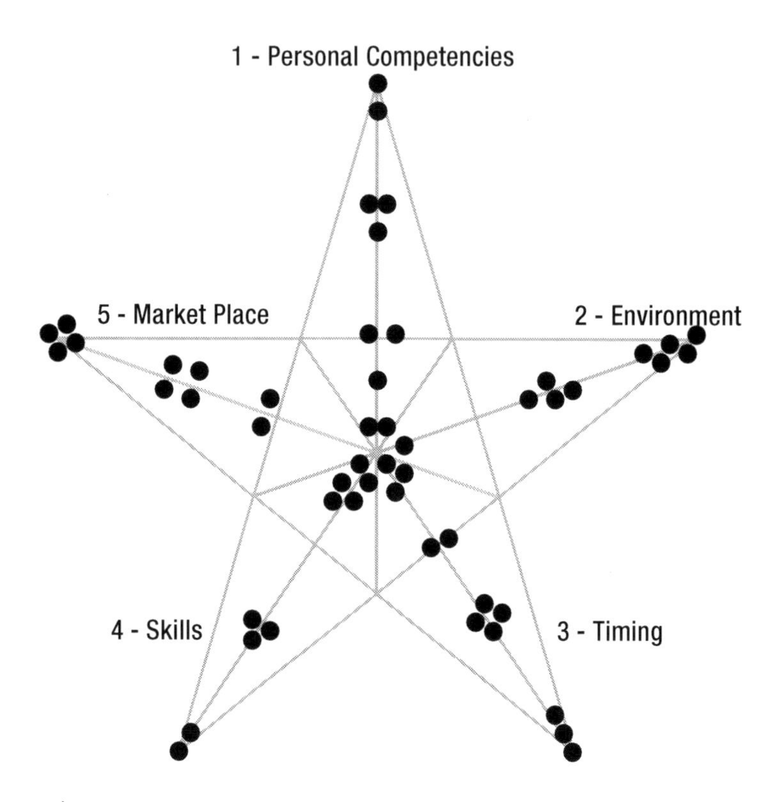

Figure 5.5 | Star Chart Assessment Results

Within the star is the shape of a pentagon (Figure 5.6). Assessment answers plotted within the pentagon represent your strengths. These strengths must be captured and are items to be exploited in your job search and interviews. Assessment answers plotted outside of the pentagon suggest that these are potential areas important to improve, and to be transferred to your personal strategic roadmap discussed in step three. Once the analysis of your assessment answers has been completed, you are ready to move on to creating your personal strategic roadmap.

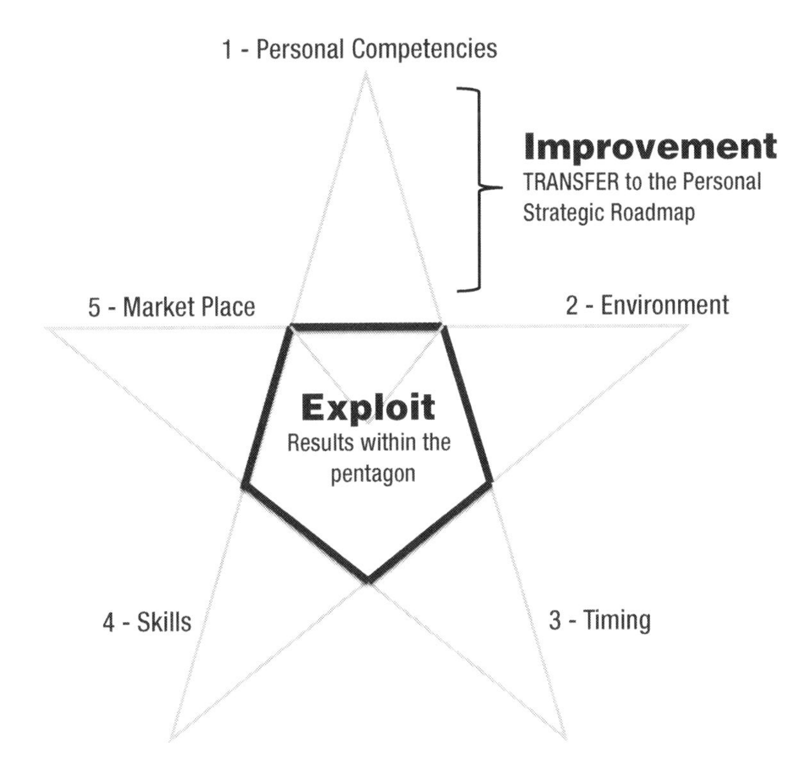

Figure 5.6 | Star Chart Areas for Improvement and Exploitation

Step Three - Setting your Goals

Next, use the personal strategic roadmap to capture your noted areas of improvement from the assessments and increase your probability of transition success. The outcome of this step will be the personal strategic roadmap shown in **Appendix E.** A full size, editable personal strategic roadmap is also available in the free online companion guide. There are four main sections to the roadmap as shown in Figure 5.7.

Personal Strategic Roadmap Sections	
1.	Improvements
2.	Vision
3.	Goals and Success
4.	Commit and Attest

Figure 5.7 | Strategic Roadmap Improvements

Use the personal strategic roadmap to list your goals and establish how you will achieve these goals, along with setting the target timeframes for each goal. It is on your roadmap that you will track and monitor these goals until achieved. You will need to monitor your goals on a recurring basis and track your progress. As goals are met, reward yourself, remove each of them from the roadmap and transfer each of these goals to your resume or exploit during your next interview.

Follow the next repeatable actions to complete each critical section of the roadmap and gain the full benefit.

Personal Strategic Road Map v1.0

IMPROVEMENTS

Vision: Obtain A Project Management career th

Vision: Obtain a career in cybersecurity.

Mission: Develop a course of action to transition into cybersecurity field.

ASSESSMENT RESULTS →	Areas for Change/Improvemen **Change / Improvement #1**
1. Environmental/Spousal	
2. Characteristics	
3. Timing	
4. Skills	Get my Certified Information Systems Security (CISSP) by November!
5. Market Place ❑ **Commercial** ❑ **Contract** ❑ **Civil Service**	

Figure 5.8 | Strategic Map Improvements

a. Capture improvements: As mentioned in step 2, identify all assessment answers outside of the pentagon. Transfer these improvements to the top portion of the roadmap in the improvements section. It is important to capture all improvements from all assessments. For example, plotted results from the skills assessment gem determine a need to achieve a commercial logistics certification. In the improvements section of the personal strategic roadmap, list those items in part 4, *skills* as shown in Figure 5.8 below:

b. State your personal vision: Based upon your reading and the improvements captured from Section 1, reflect upon how you desire to work on these improvements. Some of the improvements might be independent of others, such as your interest to take a class to achieve a certification. Some improvements might be best combined with others. For example, you may desire to focus your job search in the Civil Service market place *and* geographically target your job search to the Northeast region of the United States where you can be close to a major airport. To adequately capture the influences in achieving your personal vision, write what you want to achieve with the qualifiers that are important to you in the vision section. Include some or all of the following: Job place/location (CONUS/OCONUS, state, city), timeframe, marketplace focus, salary range, possible positions, risk level you are willing to take, industries, and any other considerations. An example is given in Figure 5.9 below:

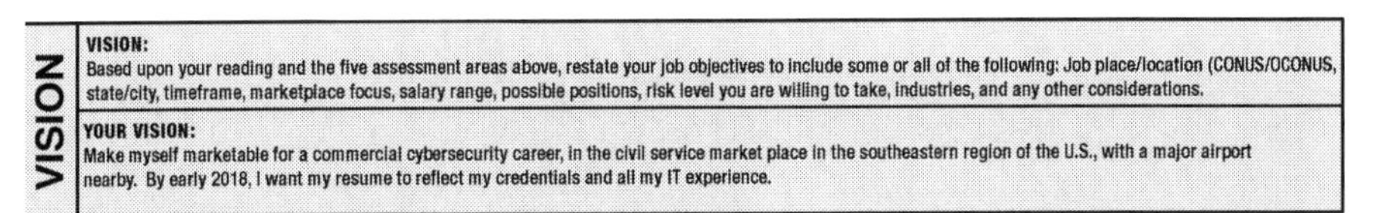

Figure 5.9 | Strategic Map Vision

c. Create goals and identify success: Now you will create goals from your areas of improvement. If there are more than four improvements, it is recommended that you focus on three or four most important to you. Further, take into consideration the level of effort and time associated with the success of achieving the goal. Some improvement/goals might be independent of one another, such as your interest to take a class to achieve a certification. Some improvement/

goals might be best grouped with one or more improvements to clarify and better define success. Transform your improvements into goals that can be achieved with an identified timeframe and measured. For example, transform the improvement 'get a cybersecurity certification' to the goal of obtaining the '(ISC)2 Certified Information Systems Security Professional (CISSP)'. Post the steps you need to take to achieve the goal, as well as a specific timeframe that you want to achieve the goal as shown in Figure 5.10 below.

GOALS & ACHIEVEMENT

GOALS:
Pick most important improvement areas from above you want to focus on, depending on level of complexity, learning, or duration (i.e., school).
*List: goals, align which Assessment it ties, year/quarter/month expected to achieve, and present your achievement path (how you will get to your goal and possible

PRIORITY	GOAL STATEMENT	ASSESSMENT TIE	PATH TO ACHIEVING GOAL	YEAR/QTR/MO TO ACHIEVE (personally set)				ACHIEVED?
GOAL #1	*CISSP Certification*	__ Environment __ Characteristics __ Timing __ Skills __ Market Place	*I will research classes available free of charge from military and other organizations, study, apply for certification, take the exam and pass!*	*03-2015* *Class*	*04-2015* *Application*	*01-2016* *Take Exam*	*Update* *Resume with* *New Cert*	YES / NO Reschedule or no longer need Date ______
GOAL #2		__ Environment __ Characteristics __ Timing __ Skills __ Market Place						YES / NO Reschedule or no longer need Date ______
GOAL #3		__ Environment __ Characteristics __ Timing __ Skills __ Market Place						YES / NO Reschedule or no longer need Date ______
GOAL #4		__ Environment __ Characteristics __ Timing __ Skills __ Market Place						YES / NO Reschedule or no longer need Date ______

Figure 5.10 | Strategic Map Goals and Achievement

Set a reminder through your calendar to review your progress on each goal listed. Depending on the urgency of the goal, review your roadmap weekly. Do this religiously and do not falter. Look at your roadmap and ask yourself – "What progress or steps have I taken to move towards achieving this goal?" Once progress is achieved, make notes in the path to achieving goal. If there are outside circumstances that have caused a slip to the right of your scheduled achievement – annotate and move on. Ask yourself was it a slip based upon not working to achieve the goal, or an outside circumstance that was out of your control? Assess the situation and adjust your goal schedule accordingly in the 'year/quarter/month to achieve area. If you achieve the goal – mark 'yes' and celebrate! You are that much closer to an easier and successful transition.

d. Commit and attest: Once you identify what you want to do, annotate it, then sign and date the roadmap as shown in Figure 5.11 below. If you have a family member or a mentor you want to watch and monitor with you, get them to co-sign. Why? You need to remind yourself and your family that you are committed to achieving these goals and that you want to remain accountable. Make a copy of this form and hang it on your refrigerator, or keep it in your wallet. Remind yourself and your family that everyone is working together on achieving these goals. Set a repeatable time for a thorough review of your personal strategic roadmap, preferably with the cosigner and revisit the courses of actions if necessary.

While this is a roadmap that captures the steps you need to transition from the military, the goals themselves are not cast in stone. If for some reason a goal becomes overcome by events, do not see this as a failure. Carefully assess the situation and the circumstances surrounding the reason why the goal is not achievable and take it off the list. Revisit sections A through D and transform other improvement areas as they develop into goals. Through achieving these goals, you will increase your 'knowns', thereby increasing your opportunity for job transition and success.

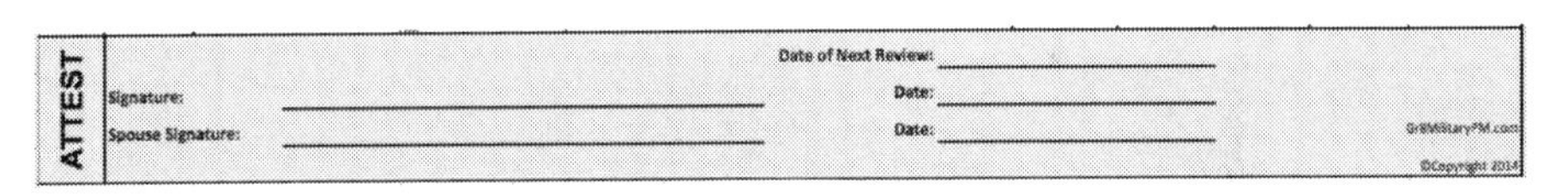
ATTEST

Date of Next Review: ____________

Signature: ____________ Date: ____________

Spouse Signature: ____________ Date: ____________

©Copyright 2014

Figure 5.11 | Strategic Map Sign and Attest

Summary

In this chapter, you gain an understanding of your strengths and weaknesses as identified in the assessments provided earlier in the book. These weaknesses are marked for improvement and are translated into goals and annotated in the personal strategic roadmap. Your strengths become areas to highlight on a resume and in an interview.

The bottom line is to increase your "knowns" and reduce the risk of the "unknowns" through preparation, planning and analysis. The more assessment results within the pentagon, the higher probability that you are ready to transition with minimum issues and stress. Use your strategic roadmap to achieve areas of improvement and increase your personal "knowns". This actionable exercise will increase the probability of success as you look and interview for jobs in the right market place that best fits you!

Many external resources, models, examples and anecdotes are provided for your consideration throughout this book. It is up to you to select and use the tools that best fit your situation. Transitioning from the military is never easy, but if you can find some nuggets within this book that you can use, then the book will have fulfilled its purpose. Finally, just know you are not alone. Many have come before you and have made the transition. Draw upon others to assist you with their transitional stories through Gr8MilitaryCyber.com. Just like the case study below, you can and will be successful in the next exciting phase of your life – plan on it!

Leroy Hall
Continuing to Grow

LEROY HALL "WANTED TO BREAK THE CYCLE OF POVERTY", so he joined the Marine Corps and was trained as a Communication Center Operator (MOS 2542). When at his first duty location on Okinawa Japan, he was assigned to the 3rd Landing Support Battalion as an IT Marine. After four years, he made a lateral move to a Marine Air/Ground Task Force Planner, but found it was not as described by his leadership and the job was less about IT and Networking and more about Force Deployment Planning and Execution. However, Leroy was able to make the best of the situation and gained experience in operating and administering Solaris and other Unix operating systems.

Over time, and with the active support of some dedicated mentors, Leroy completed his Associates Degree from East Coast Polytechnic Institute College of Technology in Virginia Beach and later attended Darton College in Georgia where he also obtained a 2-year networking support specialist certificate.This motivated him to attend a five-day CISSP boot camp in Ft Lauderdale, Florida and obtain that certificate.

With his background, Leroy was able to successfully move into the Information Assurance (IA) Specialist field (MOS 0689). He was transferred to 9th Communication Battalion where he deployed twice to Iraq as an IA Chief, followed by a transfer to the Marine Corps Network Operations and Security Center (MCNOSC) in Quantico, Virginia. After his tour at MCNOSC, he was transferred to Manpower and Reserve Affairs (M&RA) to serve as the enlisted assignments monitor for the Cybersecurity and Cyber Networking primary military occupational specialties. While he notes that he had some hardships in his early life, Leroy learned the value of education from his mother and of perseverance from the Marine Corps, often finding opportunities to expand his knowledge and experience in cybersecurity.

Currently at Marine Corps Headquarters in the Cybersecurity Division, Master Gunnery Sergeant (MGySgt) Leroy Hall recently obtained a Bachelor's degree in Information Systems Security, and is focusing on his next goal of obtaining a Master's Degree in Cybersecurity and certifications in Penetration Testing and Ethical Hacking in preparation for his upcoming retirement in August 2017.

Appendix

Appendix A – Lexicon

These selected terms are taken from the Committee on National Security Systems (CNSS) Glossary, CNSS 4009, dated 26 April 2015. CNSS 4009 provides the common lexicon for the Federal government for all terms and phrases with authoritative references related to telecommunications, system, and cyber topic. To download your own complete version, go to the CNSS site at www.cnss.gov/CNSS/issuances/Instructions.cfm

Cybersecurity

Prevention of damage to, protection of, and restoration of computers, electronic communications systems, electronic communications services, wire communication, and electronic communication, including information contained therein, to ensure its availability, integrity, authentication, confidentiality, and nonrepudiation.

Cyberspace

The interdependent network of IT infrastructures, and includes the Internet, telecommunications networks, computer systems, and embedded processors and controllers in critical industries.

Cyberspace attack

Cyberspace actions that create various direct denial effects (i.e., degradation, disruption, or destruction) and manipulation that leads to denial that is hidden or that manifests in the physical domains.

Cyberspace capability

A device, computer program, or technique, including any combination of software, firmware, or hardware, designed to create an effect in or through cyberspace.

Cyberspace defense

Actions normally created within DoD cyberspace for securing, operating, and defending the DoD information networks. Specific actions include protect, detect, characterize, counter, and mitigate.

Cyberspace operations (CO)

The employment of cyberspace capabilities where the primary purpose is to achieve objectives in or through cyberspace.

Data

Information in a specific representation, usually as a sequence of symbols that have meaning.

Defense-in-depth

Information Security strategy integrating people, technology, and operations capabilities to establish variable barriers across multiple layers and missions of the organization.

Defensive cyberspace operations (DCO)

Passive and active cyberspace operations intended to preserve the ability to utilize friendly cyberspace capabilities and protect data, networks, net-centric capabilities, and other designated systems.

Defensive cyberspace operation response action (DCO-RA)

Deliberate, authorized defensive measures or activities taken outside of the defended network to protect and defend Department of Defense (DoD) cyberspace capabilities or other designated systems.

Domain

An environment or context that includes a set of system resources and a set of system entities that have the right to access the resources as defined by a common security policy, security model, or security architecture.

Encryption certificate

A certificate containing a public key that can encrypt or decrypt electronic messages, files, documents, or data transmissions, or establish or exchange a session key for these same purposes. Key management sometimes refers to the process of storing protecting and escrowing the private component of the key pair associated with the encryption certificate.

Appendix B – Rosetta Stone

CERTIFICATION	ROLE	TOPICS OR MAJOR SKILLS COVERED/EVALUATED (AKA DOMAINS)			
Security+	Minimum requirement for most System/ Server Admins or Help Desk	Practitioner certification demonstrates basic understanding of security; Network Security; Compliance and Operational Security; Threats and Vulnerabilities		Application, Data, and Host Security; Access Control and Identity Management; Cryptography	
Certified Ethical Hacker (CEH)	CND specific certification Any role where knowledge of attack/defense techniques is needed Auditors Penetration Testers	Ethical Hacking; Footprinting & Reconnaissance; Enumeration; Scanning networks; System hacking	AMalware Evading IDS Sniffing Social Engineering Denial of Service	Session Hijacking Hacking web servers and applications SQL Injection hacking Wireless networks	Hacking mobile platforms Cloud Computing Cryptography
Certified Information System Security Professional (CISSP)	Practitioner or managerial certification demonstrating an advanced understanding of security; Allows for all IAT and IAM roles	Security and Risk Management Asset Security Security Engineering Communications and Network Security		Identity and Access Management Security Assessment and Testing Security Operations Software Development Security	
CompTia Advanced Security Professional (CASP)	Practitioner certification demonstrates advanced understanding of security; Can qualify for all technical roles, most management and most IASAE roles	Enterprise Security Risk Management, Policy/Procedure and Legal Research and Analysis Integration of Computing, Communications, and Business Disciplines			

ROLE	GENERAL REQUIREMENTS	KEY ACTIONS
Information Assurance Technician (IAT)	Primarily technical focused Privileged Access Operational positions	IATs are responsible for finding and fixing unprotected vulnerabilities and troubleshooting and testing hardware and software IA problems.
Information Assurance Managers (IAM)	Primarily management, strategy and governance focused Operational/Support positions	IAMs are responsible for the implementation and operation of a DoD IS and ensures IA related IS are functional and secure and the development and implementation of IS standards and procedures.
Computer Network Defense -Service Provider (CND-SP)	Specializes in an aspect of operational security. These areas are: - Analysis (CND-A) - Auditing (CND-AU) - Incident Response (CND-IR) - Infrastructure Support (CND-IS) - CND Management (CND-SPM)	- (CND-A) uses tools to analyze events, event information, or perform threat or target analysis - (CND-AU) performs assessments of systems and networks to identify where systems/networks deviate from acceptable configurations or policies. Evaluations may be passive (audits) or active (penetration testing) - (CND-IR) investigates and analyzes all response activities related to cyber incidents - (CND-IS) tests, implements, deploys, maintains and administers infrastructure systems required to manage the CND-SP network - (CND-SPM) oversees the CND-SP operations within the organization. Responsible for producing guidance, assisting with risk assessments and risk management, and managing the technical aspects of the defense of a network
Information System Security Architect & Engineer (ISSAE)	Specializes in security implementation through: - Architecture - Engineering	- Design, development, implementation, and/or integration of an IA architecture, system, or system component. - Ensure IA related IS will be functional and secure

Appendix C – Credentialing Options

Information Security Certifications

Certificate of Cloud Security Knowledge (CCSK)

Issuing Organization.: Cloud Security Alliance

Description: The Cloud Security Alliance has developed a widely adopted catalogue of security best practices, the Security Guidance for Critical Areas of Focus in Cloud Computing, V3. In addition, the European Network and Information Security Agency (ENISA) whitepaper, Cloud Computing: Benefits, Risks and Recommendations for Information Security is an important contribution to the cloud security body of knowledge. The Certificate of Cloud Security Knowledge (CCSK) provides evidence that an individual has successfully completed an examination covering the key concepts of the CSA guidance and ENISA whitepaper.

More information: ccsk.cloudsecurityalliance.org/

Certified Information Systems Professional (CISSP)

Issuing Organization: Information Systems Security Certification Consortium (ISC)2

Description: The CISSP is a certification for information security professionals and for the purpose of recognizing individuals who have distinguished themselves as an experienced, knowledgeable, and proficient information security practitioner. The CISSP certificate also provides a means of identifying those persons who subscribe to a rigorous requirement for maintaining their knowledge and proficiency in the information security profession.

Requirements: Candidates must have a minimum of 5 years of paid full-time work experience in 2 of the 8 domains of the CISSP Common Body of Knowledge (CBK), which covers critical topics in security including risk management, cloud computing, mobile security, application development security, and more. Certification is awarded to those individuals who achieve a prescribed level of information security experience, comply with a professional code of ethics, and pass a rigorous examination on the Common Body of Knowledge of information security. In order to maintain currency in the field, each CISSP must be recertified every three years by participation in research or study, attendance at recognized subject-matter training and professional educational programs, presentation or publication of information security papers, contributions to the information security Common Body of Knowledge, and service in professional organizations.

More information: www.isc2.org/cissp/default.aspx/

Systems Security Certification Practitioner (SSCP)
Issuing Org.: (ISC)2

Description: SSCP Certification was designed to recognize an international standard for practitioners of information security [IS] and understanding of a Common Body of Knowledge (CBK). It focuses on practices, roles and responsibilities as defined by experts from major IS industries. Certification can enhance an IS career and provide added credibility. Seven SSCP information systems security test domains are covered in the examination pertaining to the Common Body of Knowledge: Access Controls, Administration, Audit and Monitoring, Risk, Response and Recovery, Cryptography, Data Communications, Malicious Code/Malware

Requirements: Candidate is required to have a minimum of one year of cumulative paid full-time work experience in one or more of the seven domains of the SSCP CBK. If candidates do not have the required experience, they may still sit for the exam and become an Associate of (ISC)^2 until they have gained the required experience.

Endorsement - Once a candidate has been notified they have successfully passed the SSCP examination, he or she will be required to have his or her application endorsed before the credential can be awarded. The endorser attests that the candidate's assertions regarding professional experience are true to the best of their knowledge, and that the candidate is in good standing within the information security industry.

Audit – Passing candidates will be randomly selected and audited by $(ISC)^2$ Services prior to issuance of any certificate. Multiple certifications may result in a candidate being audited more than once.

More information: www.isc2.org/sscp/default.aspx

Global Information Assurance Certification (GIAC)
Issuing Organization: SANS Institute

Description: Designed to serve the people who are or will be responsible for managing and protecting important information systems and networks. GIAC course specifications & combine the opinions, knowledge, and expertise of many of the world's most experienced front-line security and system administrators, intrusion detection analysts, consultants, auditors, and managers. GIAC offers over 20 certifications in security administration, management, legal, audit, forensics, and software security. GIAC certifications align with individual job based disciplines and typically correspond to topics presented in SANS full 5-6 day courses. GIAC certification attempts have a 4 month time frame.

Requirements: There are no official prerequisites to take the GIAC certifications. Any candidate who feels that he or she has the knowledge and ability to pass the certification requirements may take the certification; however, students should be aware of the technical level of the course they wish to take. The 500 level courses are more advanced than the 400 and the 400 more advanced than the 300.

More *information:* www.giac.org/

Certified Information Security Manager (CISM)
Issuing Org.: ISACA

Description: Awarded by the Information Systems Audit and Control Association, this certification and is specifically geared toward experienced information security professionals. CISM is business-oriented and focused on information risk management while addressing management, design and technical security issues at the conceptual level. It is for the individual who must maintain a view of the big picture by managing, designing, overseeing and assessing an enterprise's information security. Requirements: Five years of work experience in the field of information security, with at least three years in the role of information security manager, successfully complete the CISM Examination, adhere to the Information Systems Audit and Control Association's Code of Professional Ethics, and submit verified evidence of a minimum of five (5) years of information security work experience, with a minimum of three (3) years of information security management work experience in three or more the CISM job practice areas

More information: www.isaca.org/Pages/default.aspx

CompTIA Security+ Certification
Issuing Org.: CompTIA

Description: CompTIA Security+ validates knowledge of systems security, network infrastructure, access control, assessments and audits, cryptography and organizational security.

Requirements: Although not a prerequisite, it is recommended that CompTIA Security+ candidates have at least two years of on-the-job technical networking experience, with an emphasis on security. The CompTIA Network+ certification is also recommended. More information: certification.comptia.org/getCertified/certifications/security.aspx

Certified CISO (C|CISO)
Issuing Org.: EC Council

Description: The certification program is aimed at producing top-level information security executives. The CCISO does not focus solely on technical knowledge but on the application of information security management principles from an executive management point of view. The program was developed by sitting CISOs for current and aspiring CISOs.

Requirements: In addition to the training requirements (waivers are offered for those holding relevant doctoral degrees) candidates must have 5 years of

IS management experience in 3 of the 5 CCISO Domains and pass the CCISO examination.

More information: ciso.eccouncil.org/cciso-certification/

Open Source Security Testing Methodology Manual (OSSTMM) Professional Security Analyst (OPSA)

Issuing Organization: ISECOM (Institute for Security and Open Methodologies). ISECOM is an open community and a non-profit organization officially registered in Catalonia, Spain. ISECOM maintains offices in Barcelona, Spain and in New York, USA.

Description: The OPSA is a certification of applied knowledge designed to improve the work done as a professional security analyst in data network security analysis, the discipline which covers critical security evaluations and decision-making required in both technical and management fields.

Requirements: Candidates will complete 50 answers of the exam within 4 hours. While it is an open book exam, no communication of any type is allowed. Each question is in the format of multiple-choice single-answer. The exam combines paper-based questions with a log files, packet captures, tool outputs, and reports. Each answer requires the accompanied data. OPSA certification requires a grade of D (60%) or better [on the relevant exam]. Each certificate is accompanied by a transcript which reflects the grade and areas of strengths and weaknesses. The grade of A (90% or better) includes a seal of excellence.

More information: www.isecom.org/certification/opsa.html

Certified Ethical Hacker (CEH) Issuing Organization. EC Council

Description: The goal of the ethical hacker is to help the organization take preemptive measures against malicious attacks by attacking the system himself; all the while staying within legal limits. The CEH Program certifies individuals in the specific network security discipline of Ethical Hacking from a vendor-neutral perspective. CEHv9 (version as of the date this was written) is a comprehensive Ethical Hacking and Information Systems Security Auditing program, suitable for candidates who want to acquaint themselves with the latest security threats, advanced attack vectors, and practical real time demonstrations of the latest hacking techniques, methodologies, tools, tricks, and security measures.

Requirements: Must attend official training or have at least two years of information security related experience and pass the CEH exam 312-50 (125 questions, 4 hours, 70% passing score)

More information: www.eccouncil.org/Certification/certified-ethical-hacker

EC-Council Certified Security Analyst (ECSA)
Issuing Organization. EC Council

Description: This certification helps analysts validate the analytical phase of ethical hacking by being able to analyze the outcome of hacking tools and technologies. By making use of innovational network penetration testing methods and techniques, an ECSA can perform the intensive assessments required to effectively identify and mitigate risks to the information security of the infrastructure. The ECSA certification is designed for candidates who are Network Server Administrators, Firewall Administrators, Information Security Testers, System Administrators and Risk Assessment Professionals.

Requirements: Complete the ECSAv9 testing process by conducting a detailed penetration test through the EC-Council iLabs Cyber range environment and submitting a written report via EC-Council's ASPEN system, then completing a multiple choice exam (150 questions, 4 hours, 70% passing score).

More information: www.eccouncil.org/about-ec-council-certified-security-analyst

Licensed Penetration Tester (LPT)
Issuing Organization: EC Council

Description: EC-Council's Licensed Penetration Tester (LPT) (Master) practical exam is the capstone to EC-Council's entire information security track; from the Certified Ethical Hacker Program (CEH) to the EC-Council Certified

Security Analyst (ECSA) Program. It all culminates with the ultimate test of your career as a penetration tester – the Licensed Penetration Tester practical exam.

Requirements: Achieve Certified Ethical Hacker (CEH) Certification, Achieve EC-Council Certified Security Analyst (ECSA) certification, Complete LPT Training Criteria (Submit LPT Application form, provide documentation on criminal background check or an authentication from an investigation agency absolving a criminal history, provide a resume with detailed professional experience, previous certification /certificates and references for verification to be submitted, and agree to EC-Council Code of Ethics), Attend LPT Workshop at selected EC-Council's Accredited Training Centers

More information: www.eccouncil.org/about-licensed-penetration-tester

Professional in Critical Infrastructure Protection (PCIP) (formerly CCISP)
Issuing Organization: Critical Infrastructure Institute

Description: Provides a strategic perspective of Critical Infrastructure Protection (CIP) in order to provide complete coverage of the CIP specialty. Critical infrastructure is defined by the office of Homeland Security as those assets, facilities, industries, and capabilities that are needed to support commerce and our daily lives. This includes SCADA, energy, utility, oil & gas, financial, communications, and transportation to name a few. The course is divided into four segments. Both the Program and Technical Courses must be completed, in sequence, before the CIP Applied Course may be undertaken.

Requirements: Completed the CIP Program Course, CIP Technical Course, and CIP Applied Course. Individual class certificates will be award upon completion of each class but the PCIP certification is only awarded upon successful completion of all three (3) classes.

More information: ci-institute.com/PCIPProgram.html

Qualified Information Assurance Professional (Q/IAP)
Issuing Organization: Security University

Description: Q/IAP Qualified/ Information Assurance Professional Certificate Program supports those individuals who are computer information security and information assurance professionals, Threat Assessment teams, Computer Security Incident Response Team (CSIRT) members, Network Security Architects and network Defense Technical Staff, and other information assurance practitioners who are involved in cybersecurity functions.

Requirements: Successfully pass Security University's Q/ISP online 125 question certification exam or all the 4 Q/ISP classes & exam. Q/ISP Certification is obtained through Security University for the purpose of recognizing qualified individuals who have distinguished themselves as knowledgeable and proficient information security practitioners with validated hands-on tactical security skills. The Q/ISP certificate also provides the means of identifying and certifying qualified persons who subscribe to a rigorous requirement for maintaining their knowledge and proficiency in information security with "validated" their hands-on tactical security skills.

More information: www.securityuniversity.net/

Certified Wireless Security Professional (CWSP)

Issuing Organization: Certified Wireless Network Professional (CWNP), a non-profit organization that sets the IT industry standard for vendor-neutral enterprise Wi-Fi certification and training.

Description: Currently, CWNP focuses on 802.11 wireless networking technologies and offers 6 levels (Entry to Expert levels) of career certification for Enterprise Wi-Fi in areas including fundamentals, administration, security, analysis, design, mastery and instruction. The CWSP certification is a professional level wireless LAN certification that ensures candidates have the skills to successfully secure enterprise Wi-Fi networks from hackers, without dependency on the brand of Wi-Fi gear deployed in the organization.

Requirements: Applicant must hold a current and valid Certified Wireless Network Administrator (CWNA) credential, and successfully complete the CWSP-205 exam.

More information: www.cwnp.com/certifications/cwsp

Physical Security and Loss Prevention Certifications

Certified Protection Professional (CPP)

Issuing Org: ASIS International

Description: The credential provides demonstrable proof of knowledge and management skills in eight key domains of security. Those who earn the CPP are ASIS board-certified in security management. Requirements: Nine years of security experience, including at least three years in responsible charge of a security function, or a Bachelor's degree or higher from an accredited institution, and seven years of security experience, including at least three years in responsible charge of a security function. (Responsible charge is defined as the charge exercised by an individual in a management position who makes decisions for the successful completion of objectives without reliance upon directions from a superior as to specific methods. However, an applicant need not have held a supervisory position, as long as the positions on which the application relies have specifically included responsibility for independent decisions or actions. If "responsible charge" is not based on supervisory responsibilities, then security program management responsibilities and duties must be clearly shown. Generally, this excludes such positions as patrol officer or the equivalent.) Candidates must also pass the CPP examination (225 questions) and have no prior conviction of significant criminal offense.

More information: www.asisonline.org/Certification/Board-Certifications/CPP/Pages/default.aspx

Physical Security Professional (PSP)

Issuing Org.: ASIS International

Description: Provides demonstrated knowledge and experience in threat assessment and risk analysis; integrated physical security systems; and the appropriate identification, implementation, and ongoing evaluation of security measures. Those who earn the PSP are ASIS board certified in physical security. Requirements: High school diploma, GED equivalent, or associate degree and six years of progressive physical security experience or a bachelor's degree or higher and four years of progressive physical security experience. (Physical security is defined as the various physical measures designed to safeguard personnel, property, and information. Progressive means that the experience has included increasingly more difficult assignments or responsibilities over the work period). Candidate must also pass the PSP examination (140 questions).

More information: www.asisonline.org/Certification/Board-Certifications/PSP/Pages/default.aspx

Professional Certified Investigator (PCI)

Issuing Organization.: ASIS International

Description: Provides demonstrable proof of an individual's knowledge and experience in case management, evidence collection, and preparation of reports and testimony to substantiate findings. Those who earn the PCI are ASIS board-certified in investigations.

Requirements: High school diploma or GED equivalent and five years of investigations experience with at least two years in case management. Case management is the coordination and direction of an investigation utilizing various disciplines and resources, the findings of which would be assessed to establish the facts/findings of the investigation as a whole; the management process of investigation More information: www.asisonline.org/Certification/Board-Certifications/PCI/Pages/default.aspx

Loss Prevention Qualified (LPQ)

Issuing Organization: Loss Prevention Foundation

Description: Designed to be a benchmark education for entry-level loss prevention professionals, such as loss prevention managers, supervisors, store managers, college students, select hourly employees, or for those who are interested in entering the loss prevention profession. Requirements: The exam is composed of 100 multiple-choice questions and is offered on a regular basis and select locations throughout the country. All exams are offered in a computer-based format and are proctored. One does not have to complete the LPQ course before taking the exam, however it is highly recommended.

More information: www.losspreventioncertification.com/INDX-LearnMore.htm

Loss Prevention Certified (LPC)

Issuing Organization: Loss Prevention Foundation

Description: A certification that was designed as advanced education for loss prevention management and executives who hope to further their career in the loss prevention field.."

Requirements: Online coursework and proctored exam.

More information: www.losspreventioncertification.com/INDX-LearnMore.htm

Certified Fraud Examiner (CFE)

Issuing Organization: Association of Certified Fraud Examiners

Description: The Certified Fraud Examiner program is an accrediting process for individuals with the specialized skills to detect, investigate, and deter fraud. Certified Fraud Examiners have the expertise to resolve allegations of fraud from inception to disposition, gather evidence, take statements, write reports, testify to findings, and assist in the prevention and detection of fraud.

Requirements: Be an Associate member of the ACFE in good standing, Have a minimum of two years professional experience and 50 points. Successfully pass the exam. Be of high moral character. Agree to abide the bylaws and Code of Professional Ethics of the Association of Certified Fraud Examiners. Points claimed for education must be from a recognized institution of higher learning. If an individual has more than 40 but less than 50 total qualifying points, the individual may apply to take the CFE Exam; however, certification will not be awarded until the individual has a total of 50 points or more and two years of professional experience. Points are determined from years of experience, college level (years attended or degrees), and other certifications.

More information: www.acfe.com/become-cfe-qualifications.aspx

Certified Identity Theft Risk Management Specialist (CITRMS)
Issuing Org: Institute of Consumer Financial Education

Description: The main purpose is to comprehensively prepare and equip law enforcement professionals, financial planners and CPA's, resolution advocates, notaries, lawyers, credit and debt counselors, through education, testing and computer software training, with the knowledge and skills necessary to help consumers and businesses fully assess and minimize their present risk of credit and identity theft.

Requirements: Enroll, receive and completed the ICFE program materials. Using software provided, take the 100 question examination (80% passing)

More information: www.financial-education-icfe.org/identity_theft_specialist/identity_theft_risk_management_specialist_certification.asp

CyberSecurity Forensic Analyst (CSFA)
Issuing Organization: Cybersecurity Institute

Description: Certification provides proof that the analyst can conduct a thorough and sound forensic examination of a computer system and other digital/electronic devices, properly interpret the evidence, and communicate the examination results effectively and understandably.

Requirements: Minimum 2 years' experience, plus an FBI background check. Candidate takes CSFA exam (up to three days to complete) There is a written component of 50 multiple choice questions (30% of total score), with the majority of the test being hands-on practical (70% of score). Candidates will be given a scenario that includes processing a hard drive and may include other media such as a CD, DVD, or USB drive. Some scenarios include a cellular phone or other handheld device. The test candidate may be presented with a running computer to analyze, or will have the media/devices to be analyzed being delivered by courier. Hard drives to be processed will be 10 Gigabytes or smaller, depending on the scenario. An overall score of 85% must be attained in order to earn the designation of CyberSecurity Forensic Analyst (CSFA).

More information: www.cybersecurityforensicanalyst.com//index.html

Audit Certifications

Certified Information Systems Auditor (CISA)
Issuing Organization: ISACA

Description: Awarded by the Information Systems Audit and Control Association, the CISA certification is a globally recognized certification for IS audit control, assurance and security professionals. With this certification, candidates can showcase their audit experience, skills and knowledge, and demonstrate the capability to assess vulnerabilities, report on compliance and institute controls within their enterprise.

Requirements: Candidates must have five years of work experience in the fields of Information Systems Auditing, Control, Assurance or Security. Candidates must successfully complete the CISM Examination.

More information: www.isaca.org/Pages/default.aspx

Certified Internal Auditor (CIA)
Issuing Organization: Institute of Internal Auditors

Description: CIAs master auditing standards and practices as well as management principles and controls, IT, and emerging strategies to improve business and government. CIAs learn the best ways to manage business. The CIA exam tests a candidate's knowledge and ability regarding the current practice of internal auditing.

Requirements: Valid photo ID, Completion of the Internal Audit Practitioner program application, Character reference, Six months internal audit or equivalent experience (i.e., experience in audit or assessment disciplines, including internal auditing, external auditing, quality assurance, compliance, and internal control). The experience requirement must be fulfilled by the point of completion of the exams. There is no defined educational requirement.

More information: na.theiia.org/certification/cia-certification/Pages/CIA-Certification.aspx

Certification in Control Self-Assessment (CCSA)

Issuing Org: Institute of Internal Auditors Description: Gaining the required knowledge of areas such as risk and control models—often considered the realm of auditors only—exposes CSA practitioners from all backgrounds to concepts that are vital in effectively using CSA to help clients achieve their objectives.

Requirements: Candidates must complete 54 CPD (continuing professional development) hours in the following manner: 18 CPD hours for Introduction to Control Self-Assessment; 18 CPD hours for either Value-Added Business Controls: The Right Way to Manage Risk or Evaluating Internal Controls: A COSO-Based Approach; and 18 CPD hours for either Assessing Risk: A Better Way to Audit or CSA Facilitation Techniques for Auditors.". Finance Theory, Financial Instruments and Markets, Mathematical Foundations of Risk Measurement, Risk Management Practices, Case Studies, PRMIA Standards of Best Practice, Conduct and Ethics, Bylaws

More information: na.theiia.org/certification/CCSA-Certification/Pages/CCSA-Certification.aspx

Certified in Risk and Information Systems Control (CRISC)

Issuing Org: ISACA

Description: Designed for IT professionals who have hands-on experience with risk identification, assessment, and evaluation; risk response; risk monitoring; IS control design and implementation; and IS control monitoring and maintenance.

Requirements: Successful completion of the CRISC examination. A minimum of at least three years of cumulative work experience performing the tasks of a CRISC professional across at least two of the four CRISC domains is required for certification. Of these two required domains, one must be in either Domain 1—Risk Identification or 2—IT Risk Assessment. There are no substitutions or experience waivers. Experience must have been gained within the 10-year period preceding the application date for certification or within five years from the date of initially passing the examination.

More information: www.isaca.org/Certification/CRISC-Certified-in-Risk-and-Information-Systems-Control/Pages/default.aspx

Appendix D – Colleges, Universities, and Institutions

DEVELOPER	RESOURCE	URL
Anne Arundel Community College	CyberCenter	www.aacc.edu/cybercenter/
Bellevue University	Cybersecurity Degrees (BS, MS); Computer Information Systems BS Degree; Management of Information Systems MS Degree; Master of Business Administration with a concentration in Cybersecurity of Management Information Systems	www.bellevue.edu/index.aspx
Bossier Parish Community College	Prior Learning Assessment Matrix; Computer Technology Certifications	bpcc.edu/index.html
Capitol Technology University	Cybersecurity Degrees (BS, MS, DSc)	www.captechu.edu/
CERT Program	Certified Computer Security Incident Handler Certification	www.cert.org/certification/
Certified Wireless Network Professional (CWNP)	Certified Wireless Security Professional	www.cwnp.com/certifications/cwsp/
Chief Information Officers Council	2012 Clinger-Cohen Core Competencies & Learning Objectives	cio.gov/wp-content/uploads/downloads/2013/01/2012-Learning-Objectives-Final.docx
College of Southern Maryland	Information Systems Security	www.csmd.edu/BAT/TEC/InformationSystemsSecurity.htm
Community College of Baltimore County	Information Systems Security Degree and Certificate	www.ccbcmd.edu
CompTIA	CompTIA Security+; Advanced Security Practitioner; A+; Network+ Certifications	certification.comptia.org/getCertified/certifications/
Council on CyberSecurity	The Critical Security Controls for Effective Cyber Defense, Version 5.0	www.counciloncybersecurity.org/attachments/article/12/CSC-MASTER-VER50-2-27-2014.pdf
DRI International	DRI Associate Business Continuity Professional; Certified Business Continuity Professional; Certified Functional Continuity Professional; Master Business Continuity Professional Certifications	www.drii.org/certification/certification.php
EC-Council	Computer Hacking Forensic Investigator (CHFI); EC-Council Certified Security Analyst (ECSA) Certifications	cert.eccouncil.org/
Erie Community College	Information Systems Security Curriculum and Program Competencies	www.ecc.edu/academics/programs/infosystems

DEVELOPER	RESOURCE	URL
Anne Arundel Community College	CyberCenter	www.aacc.edu/cybercenter/
Francis Tuttle Technology School	Cybersecurity Curricula and Certifications	www.francistuttle.edu/classOfferings/careerTraining/pathway.aspx?PFID=60
Global Information Assurance Certification (GIAC)	GIAC Certified Incident Handler; Information Security Fundamentals; Security Essentials Certification; Security Expert; Security Leadership Certification; Systems and Network Auditor; Certified Penetration Tester Certifications	www.giac.org/certifications
Hagerstown Community College	Cybersecurity degrees and certificates	catalog.hagerstowncc.edu/content.php?catoid=2&navoid=82
Harford Community College	Information Assurance and Cybersecurity Certificate and Associate of Applied Sciences Degree	www.harford.edu/iss/default.asp
Information Assurance Certification Review Board (IACRB)	Certified Expert Penetration Tester (CEPT) Certification	www.iacertification.org/cept_certified_expert_penetration_tester.html
Information Systems Security Certification Consortium, Inc., (ISC)²	(ISC)² Certified Information Systems Security Practitioner (CISSP); Systems Security Certified Practitioner (SSCP) Certifications	www.isc2.org/credentials/default.aspx
Infotec	Security Certified Program (SCP) Security Certified Network Architect; Security Certified Program (SCP) Security Certified Network Professional Certifications	www.infotecpro.com/instructorled/certifications/security/scp.htm
Inver Hills Community College	Network Technology and Security A.A.S.	www.inverhills.edu/Departments/CNT/index.aspx#AAS
ISACA	ISACA Certified Information Security Manager; Certified Information Security Auditor Certifications	www.isaca.org/CERTIFICATION/Pages/default.aspx
Ivy Tech Community College	Computer IT A.A.S. and Certificate; Short Term Certificate in Systems Security; Short Term Certificate in Data Security; Short Term Certificate in Network Security; Information Security A.A.S. and Certificate	cc.ivytech.edu/cp/home/displaylogin
Jackson State Community College	Information Assurance A.A.S. and Multidisciplinary Discipline	www.jscc.edu/academics/disciplines/computer-information-systems/programs-of-study/information-assurance-concentration.html
Montgomery College	Cybersecurity Curricula	cms.montgomerycollege.edu/EDU/Plain.aspx?id=13043#iss
Moraine Valley Community College	IT Security Specialist - Associate in Applied Science Degree	www.morainevalley.edu/programs/2009-2010/2009-2010_fall/1420_course.htm

DEVELOPER	RESOURCE	URL
National Information Assurance Training and Education Center (NIATEC)	National Security Telecommunications and Information Systems Security National Training Standards	niatec.info/ViewPage.aspx?id=103
National Initiative for Cybersecurity Careers and Studies	National Initiative for Cybersecurity Education (NICE) Interactive National Cybersecurity Workforce Framework	niccs.us-cert.gov/research/draft-national-cybersecurity-workforce-framework-version-20
National Institute of Standards and Technology	Federal Information Security Management Act (FISMA)	csrc.nist.gov/groups/SMA/fisma/index.html
	National Cybersecurity Center of Excellence	csrc.nist.gov/nccoe/
	Framework for Improving Critical Infrastructure Cybersecurity	www.nist.gov/cyberframework/upload/cybersecurity-framework-021214-final.pdf
Office of Virginia's Secretary of Technology	Virginia's Innovation Ecosystem: The Trusted Leader in Growing Cybersecurity Solutions	www.technology.virginia.gov/CyberReport.pdf
Oklahoma City Community College	Cyber/Information Security A.A.S. and Certificate of Mastery	www.occc.edu/academics/programs/cyber-information-security.html
Owens Community College	System Security and Information Assurance Major, AAB	catalog.owens.edu/preview_program.php?catoid=3&poid=623&hl=%22ssia%22&returnto=search
Prince George's Community College	Information Security A.A.S.; Cybercrime Investigation OPT. Criminal Justice, A.A.S.; Information Security Management Certificate; Cybercrime Investigation Certificate; Information Security Certificate	www.pgcc.edu/Programs_and_Courses/Programs ___Courses.aspx
Richland College of the Dallas County Community College District	Digital Forensics A.A.S.; Information Security/Information Assurance Certificate	www.richlandcollege.edu/
Rose State College	CNSS Certification Curriculum; Cybersecurity Information – Security Certificate Program	www.rose.edu
SANS	Cyber Defense Foundations Curriculum	www.sans.org/
Sinclair Community College	Computer Information Systems; CIS/Microsoft Security Specialist A.A.S.; Cyber Investigation Technology A.A.S.; Cyber Investigation Certificate; Information Systems Security Short Term Technical Certificate; Linux Security and Network Essentials Short Term Technical Certificate	www.sinclair.edu
Snead State Community	Information Systems Security	www.snead.edu
College	(INFOSEC) Professionals Course Map; Systems Administration Course Map; Computer Science Technology A.A.S.	

DEVELOPER	RESOURCE	URL
The Committee on National Security Systems	National Training Standard for Information Systems Security Professionals	www.cnss.gov/Assets/pdf/nstissi_4011.pdf
The Committee on National Security Systems	Telecommunications Security Group (TSG) Standards	www.cnss.gov/tsg.html
The Committee on National Security Systems	National Training Standard for Information Systems Security Professionals; Telecommunications Security Group Standards; National Information Assurance Training for Senior System Managers; National Training Standard for Information Systems Security Professionals; National Information Assurance Training Standard for System Administrators; National Information Assurance Training Standards For Risk Analysts; National Training Standard for System Certifiers; National Information Assurance Training Standard for Information Systems Security Officers	www.cnss.gov
The Lexington Institute	Averting Catastrophe in Cyberspace: Core Requirements	www.northropgrumman.com/Capabilities/Cybersecurity/Documents/Literature/Averting_Catastrophe_In_Cyber.pdf
The White House	Cyberspace policy Review	www.whitehouse.gov/assets/documents/Cyberspace_Policy_Review_final.pdf
United States Department of Homeland Security	IT Security Essential Body of Knowledge	buildsecurityin.us-cert.gov/bsi/dhs/921-BSI.html
Valencia College	Cybersecurity Intro; Textbooks; Flowchart; Recommended Plan of Study; Pathways to Industry Certifications; Pathways to NSA Certifications	valenciacollege.edu
Whatcom Community College	Computer Information Systems Degree and Courses; Certificate of Proficiency - Information Security Professional; Computer Information Systems – Technical Support; Computer Information Systems – Network Administration; Office Professional Technical Support Specialist Certificate;	www.whatcom.ctc.edu

Appendix E – Personal Strategic Roadmap

Personal Strategic Road Map v1.0 GR8MilitaryPM ©

Vision: Obtain A Project Management career that meets or exceeds my expectations

Mission: Develop a course of action to create a satisfying and financially lucrative transitional outcome.

Transition Date:

RoadMap Initiation Date:

IMPROVEMENTS

ASSESSMENT RESULTS → Areas for Change/Improvement from Star Chart results *outside the pentagon*	Change / Improvement # 1	Change / Improvement #2	Change / Improvement #3	Change / Improvement #4
1. Environmental/Spousal				
2. Characteristics				
3. Timing				
4. Skills				
5. Market Place ◻ Commercial ◻ Contract ◻ Civil Service				

VISION

VISION:

Based upon your reading and the five assessment areas above, restate your job objectives to include some or all of the following: Job place/location (CONUS/OCONUS, state/city, timeframe, marketplace focus, salary range, possible positions, risk level you are willing to take, industries, and any other considerations

YOUR VISION:

GOALS & ACHIEVEMENT

GOALS:

Pick most important improvement areas from above you want to focus on, depending on level of complexity, learning, or duration (i.e., school).

* List: goals, align which Assessment it ties, year/quarter/month expected to achieve, and present your achievement path (how you will get to your goal and possible steps if necessary

PRIORITY	GOAL STATEMENT	ASSESSMENT TIE	PATH TO ACHIEVING GOAL	YEAR/QTR/MO TO ACHIEVE (personally set)				ACHIEVED ?
GOAL # 1	*enter goal here.....*	__ Environment __ Characteristics __ Timing __ Skills __ Market Place	*enter steps.....*					YES / NO Reschedule or no longer need? Date ______
GOAL # 2		__ Environment __ Characteristics __ Timing __ Skills __ Market Place						YES / NO Reschedule or no longer need? Date ______
GOAL # 3		__ Environment __ Characteristics __ Timing __ Skills __ Market Place						YES / NO Reschedule or no longer need? Date ______
GOAL # 4		__ Environment __ Characteristics __ Timing __ Skills __ Market Place						YES / NO Reschedule or no longer need? Date ______

ATTEST

Date of Next Review: ____________________

Signature: ____________________ Date: ____________________

Spouse Signature: ____________________ Date: ____________________

GR8MilitaryPM.com

Acknowledgements

I was asked by my leadership back in 1984 while stationed with the 6912th ESG/690th ESW in Berlin if it was true that I had a new thing called a "personal computer". I replied to the affirmative and proudly described my acquisition of which I paid $3000 from my recent reenlistment bonus. It was a Zenith-100, with an 8086 processor, and a 40MB hard drive running DOS 3.0 with two (count them…two) 5.25" floppy drives. It had a whopping 64K of RAM, a color graphics adaptor (CGA) card, a color monitor, and an internal modem. "So, you know computers…congratulations!" I was told. "You are the Wing Comm-Computer Security Officer and head of the Small Computer Branch." Little could I imagine when I "fell" into the cybersecurity career field well over 30 years ago how my life was going to change…shifting from a career as an intelligence linguist and analyst to the field I work today. There are so many mentors and colleagues over the years, from both the Air Force and Marine Corps, who helped shape my understanding of information security/information assurance/cybersecurity to the depths I have today…some who are no longer with us, but whose memory I will always cherish. Because of them I have developed the depth of understanding in cybersecurity that remains my vision and stance to this day. My deepest thanks to my co-authors, Sandy Cobb and Jay Hicks, who were so patient with me in the writing of this book, particularly when so many major life issues happened during the time. Naturally, I need to acknowledge my dear family, who was so patient with me during this time, when I kept worrying about the time I needed to devote to writing. Lastly, it has always been my desire to show others how they can transition into what I believe is a rich and rewarding profession...one that is becoming more critical every passing moment. After writing this book, there are still changes in specialty names and skills happening today...and more expected to come. Just three months ago (April 2017) the Marine Corps began considering creating a new cyberspace operations MOS...17XX. Even with all the changes happening, it is my sincerest hope this book will still be of some value and assistance to all who read it and want to come into the cybersecurity field.

~ Ray A. Letteer, Stafford, VA
10 June 2017

The Transitioning Military Series

The Transitioning Military Series helps service members evaluate and understand their potential to transform themselves into a marketable commodity within both public and private sectors. Each career-based book enables the translation of military experience to the commercial world. Read and use each of these books as a reference to guide during your transition. Insight is provided for those seeking the most satisfying job beyond their military career, with real-world success stories.

A unique combination of features offered through this book series include:

- Career Mapping and Translation
- Commercial Market Exploration
- Transitional Preparedness
- Individual Assessments
- Personal Strategic Roadmap

Interested in another career field? Check out our other books on career field transition for the military:

Project Manager

Logistician

Information Technology

Jay Hicks and Sandy Cobb are dedicated to providing insight and guidance for those looking to transition successfully from the military with the least amount of stress. Both Jay and Sandy speak around the U.S. in support of transition as well as career field insight, and are available for conferences, podcasts, webinars, and training. For more information on upcoming events and new releases, visit: GR8Transitions4U.com.

End Notes

Chapter 1

1 Mark Prensky, "Digital Natives, Digital Immigrants", *On the Horizon* (MCB University Press, Vol. 9 No. 5, October 2001), *http://marcprensky.com/writing/Prensky%20-%20Digital%20Natives,%20Digital%20Immigrants%20-%20Part1.pdf* (Accessed 15 May 2016)

2 *http://csrc.nist.gov/groups/SMA/ispab/documents/DOD-Strategy-for-Operating-in-Cyberspace.pdf*

3 *https://www.performance.gov/node/3401/view?view=public*

4 *http://www.pymnts.com/news/security-and-risk/2016/inside-cybersecuritys-booming-2016-job-market/*

5 *https://www.forbes.com/sites/stevemorgan/2016/01/02/one-million-cybersecurity-job-openings-in-2016/#40f0b8f127ea*

6 *http://csrc.nist.gov/nice/NICE_Workforce_Demand.pdf*

Chapter 2

1 Christopher, Shane, "GI Jobs – Why are employers Seeking Military Experience", G.I.Jobs, April 28, 2014 (accessed July 10, 2014). *http://www.gijobs.com/employers-seeking-military-experience*

2 *http://www.showyourstripes.org/resources/top100military.html,* 2013 Top 100 Military Friendly Employers

3 *http://www.shrm.org/research/surveyfindings/documents/10-0531%20 military%20program%20report_fnl.pdf, Employing Military Personnel and Recruiting Veterans, What HR can do.* Society of Human Resource Managers (SHRM), 2010.

4 Freed, S.E. (2014). *Examination of personality characteristics among cybersecurity and information technologyIT professionals.* (Master's), University of Tennessee at Chattanooga, Chattanooga, TN. Retrieved from *http://scholar.utc.edu/cgi/viewcontent.cgi?article=1126&context=theses*

5 Boylan, M. (2009). *Basic ethics, 2nd ed.* Upper Saddle River, NJ: Pearson/Prentice Hall. ISBN-13: 978-0-13-600655-8

6 Grossman, D. (2009) *On Killing: The Psychological Cost Of Learning To Kill In War And Society* Back Bay Books, ISBN-13: 978-0-31-604093-8

7 Biro, Meghan, *"5 Reasons Leaders Hire Veterans,"* Forbes, November 4, 2012, https://www.forbes.com/sites/meghanbiro/2012/11/04/5-reasons-leaders-hire-veterans/#6989a7d54796 (accessed June 8, 2017)

8 Henry, Todd, "Die Empty", (Portfolio / Penguin NY, New York, 2013), 4.

9 Gottreu, Scott, "The Difference Between Occupation & Vocation", January 09, 2012, http://www.codeoffaith.com/804/the-difference-between-occupation-vocation, (accessed May 2, 2016).

10 Henry, Todd, "The Accidental Creative", (Portfolio / Penguin NY, New York, 2011), 210.

11 U.S Department of Veteran's Affairs, "Education and Training", *http://www.benefits.va.gov/gibill/post911_gibill.asp,* (accessed May 2, 2016).

12 Lerner, Michele, "How big should your emergency fund be?" Bankrate.com, Mar 6, 2012, http://www.bankrate.com/finance/savings/how-big-should-emergency-fund-be.aspx (accessed May 2, 2016).

13 Caarl S. Savino and Ronald L. Krannich, Ph.D., "The Military to Civilian Transition Guide, secrets to finding a great jobs and employers", (Competitive Edge Services, 2014-2015 edition), 42.

14 Doyle, Alison, "Resume Types: Chronological, Functional, Combination", About.com, 2015, *http://jobsearch.about.com/od/resumes/p/resumetypes.htm*, (accessed May 2, 2016)

15 Savino and Krannich, "The Military to Civilian Transition Guide", 10.

16 Hicks, Jay, "Bullet Proof Your Resume", LinkedIn, *https://www.linkedin.com/pulse/bullet-proof-your-resume-jay-hicks-pmp?trk=pulse_spock-articles,* (accessed May 2, 2016).

17 Hicks, Jay, "Do you have a 'Killer Cover Letter'?", LinkedIn, *https://www.linkedin.com/pulse/transitioning-military-service-members-do-you-have-cover-hicks-pmp?trk=pulse_spock-articles,* (accessed May 2, 2016).

Chapter 3

1 Moore, G. E., Cramming more components onto integrated circuits, *Electronics,* pp. 114–117, April 19, 1965. Publisher Item Identifier S 0018-9219(98)00753-1.

2 Cybrary, Cybersecurity job trends, December 2015, *https://www.cybrary.it/wp-content/uploads/2015/12/2016-Job-Trends. jpg (Accessed 16 April 2016)*

3 NIST, Early Computer Security Papers (1970-1985), Introduction, October 16, 2016, *http://csrc.nist.gov/publications/history/ (Accessed 9 Jan 2016)*

4 Gibson, W. (1984). Neuromancer, p.51, New York, NY: The Berkley Publishing Group, the Penguin Group.

5 *National strategy to secure cyberspace.* Washington, DC: Retrieved from *http://www.us-cert.gov/reading_room/cyberspace_strategy.pdf.*

6 National military strategy for cyberspace operations. Washington, DC: Joint Chiefs of Staff Retrieved from *www.dod.mil/pubs/foi/joint_staff/jointStaff.../07-F-2105doc1.pdf.*

7 *Joint publication 1-02, Department of Defense dictionary of military and related terms.* Washington DC: Joint Chiefs of Staff Retrieved

from *http://cgsc.contentdm.oclc.org/utils/getfile/collection/p4013coll9/id/610/filename/634.pdf.*

8 *Joint publication 5-0, Joint operations planning.* Washington DC: Joint Chiefs of Staff Retrieved from *http://www.dtic.mil/doctrine/new_pubs/jp5_0.pdf.*

9 Gates, R. M. (2011). *Department of Defense Strategy for Operating in Cyberspace.* Washington, DC: Retrieved from *http://www.defense.gov/news/d20110714cyber.pdf.*

10 National Initiative for Cybersecurity Education (NICE), *http://csrc.nist.gov/nice, (accessed June 8, 2017).*

11 Bush (2008) *National Security Presidential Directive (NSPD)-54/Homeland Security Presidential Security Directive (HSPD)-23*, 8 Jan 2008, Washington DC. Retrieved from *https://epic.org/privacy/cybersecurity/EPIC-FOIA-NSPD54.pdf*

12 FY13 National Defense Authorization Act, Section 933, *www.gpo.gov/fdsys/pkg/BILLS-112hr4310enr/pdf/BILLS-112hr4310enr.pdf* (Accessed 15 March 2015)

13 Framework for Improving Critical Infrastructure Cybersecurity, National Institute of Standards and Technology, February 12, 2014, *https://www.nist.gov/sites/default/files/documents/cyberframework/cybersecurity-framework-021214.pdf, (accessed June 8, 2017).*

14 Letteer, R. A. (2013). *Exploring the development of the cyber Marine: A mixed methods study of Marine Corps cyberspace operations requirements and training* (Doctor of Science, IA), Capitol College. Retrieved from *https://www.academia.edu/5335318/Examining_the_Development_of_the_Cyber_Marine*

15 Framework, National Initiative for Cybersecurity Education (NICE), *http://csrc.nist.gov/nice/framework, (accessed June 8, 2017).*

16 White House, Fact Sheet: Cybersecurity National Action Plan, February 09, 2016, *https://www.whitehouse.gov/the-press-office/2016/02/09/fact-sheet-cybersecurity-national-action-plan (accessed June 8, 2017).*

17 CyberCorps (R): Scholarship For Service (SFS), Office of Personnel Management, *https://www.sfs.opm.gov, (accessed June 8, 2017).*

18 The Federal Cybersecurity Workforce Strategy, The White House, *https://www.whitehouse.gov/sites/default/files/omb/memoranda/2016/m-16-15.pdf, no longer available with change of administration.*

19 Kenneth Corbin, "Cybersecurity Pros in High Demand, Highly Paid and Highly Selective", *http://www.cio.com/article/2383451/careers-staffing/cybersecurity-pros-in-high-demand--highly-paid-and-highly-selective.html* (Accessed 15 May 2016)

20 National Initiative for Cybersecurity Careers and Studies, *https://niccs.us-cert.gov/* (Accessed 22 March 2016)

Chapter 4

1 Tranette Ledford, "The Best Jobs: Government Employee or Government Contractor?," ClearanceJobs, July 25, 2010, http://news.clearancejobs.com/2010/07/25/the-best-jobs-government-employee-or-government-contractor (accessed February 18, 2015).

2 Tranette Ledford, "The Best Jobs: Government Employee or Government Contractor?"

3 Tranette Ledford, "The Best Jobs: Government Employee or Government Contractor?"

4 "The Best Places to Work in the Federal Government 2013 Rankings," Partnership for Public Service, June 14, 2013, *http://bestplacestowork.org/BPTW/rankings/governmentwide* (accessed February 18, 2015).

5 "The Best Places to Work in the Federal Government 2013 Rankings,"

6 *https://www.opm.gov/policy-data-oversight/pay-leave/reference-materials/handbooks/compensation-flexibilities-to-recruit-and-retain-cybersecurity-professionals.pdf*

7 *https://www.opm.gov/policy-data-oversight/classification-qualifications/general-schedule-qualification-standards/2200/information-technology-it-management-series-2210-alternative-a/* (Accessed 15 May 2016)

8 *https://www.opm.gov/policy-data-oversight/pay-leave/salaries-wages/salary-tables/pdf/2016/DCB.pdf* (Accessed 10 April 2016)

9 "Benefits, Leave, and Pay for Federal Employees," USA.Gov, February 02, 2015, *http://www.usa.gov/FederalFederalFederalFederalFederalFederal-Employees/Benefits.shtml* (accessed February 18, 2015).

10 Adam Stone, "Breaking down pros & cons of public & private sectors," Navy Times, March 26, 2014, *http://www.navytimes.com/article/20140326/JOBS/303260044/Breaking-down-pros-cons-public-private-sectors/* (accessed February 18, 2015).

11 John Cibinic, Jr. and Ralph C. Nash, Jr., Administration of Government Contracts, Third Edition, (The George Washington University, Government Contracts Program, National Law Center, Washington D.C., 1995), 3.

12 Tranette Ledford, "The Best Jobs: Government Employee or Government Contractor?"

13 Adam Stone, "Breaking down pros & cons of public & private sectors," Navy Times, March 26, 2014, http://www.navytimes.com/article/20140326/JOBS/303260044/Breaking-down-pros-cons-public-private-sectors/ (accessed February 18, 2015).

14 401(k) Plans," Internal Revenue Service, October 14, 2014, *http://www.irs.gov/Retirement-Plans/401(k)-Plans* (accessed February 18, 2015).

15 The Consultants' Corner, "The Stark difference between private and public sector ERP implementations, Panorama Consulting Solutions, September 13, 2013, *http://panorama-consulting.com/the-stark-difference-between-private-and-public-sector-erp-implementations/* (accessed February 18, 2015).

16 "Report of the Federal Salary Council Working Group," GovernmentExecutive.com, September, 2014, *http://www.govexec.com/media/gbc/docs/pdfs_edit/101714kl2.pdf* (accessed February 18, 2015).

17 Richard Morgan, "Five Mandatory Benefits for Full-Time Employees," Houston Chronicle, *http://smallbusiness.chron.com/five-mandatory-benefits-fulltime-employees-18874.html* (accessed February 18, 2015).

18 "PricewaterhouseCoopers, LLP," Great Place to Work® Institute, November 11, 2014, *http://us.greatrated.com/pwc/great-perks* (accessed February 18, 2015).

19 "The Best Places to Work in the Federal Government 2013 Rankings."

Made in the USA
Columbia, SC
22 July 2017